DOS GRINGOS

A Norwegian and an Irishman
meet in a Texas bar…

"From a true story during The Mexican Revolution"

FREDERICK R. ANDRESEN

Dos Gringos
A Norwegian and an Irishman meet in a Texas bar…
From a true story set in the Mexican Revolution

Aviara Press

ISBN: 978-0-9965020-2-3

My thanks…

So many have helped me prepare this story for sharing. Returning to my home town of El Paso I was greatly helped by Claudia Rivers and her staff at the Archives of the University of Texas at El Paso where I could verify important historical details. Danny Gonzalez at the El Paso Public Library and the staff there was helpful in research and photos of the time and area. And important contributions were made in my Master Class at the Taos Writer's Conference with John Dufresne, as well as by Barnaby Conrad. The final edit was by Sara Joyce Robinson and earlier edits and helpful suggestions along the way came from Loretta Hudson, Jennifer Silva Redmond, Teresa Cullen, and my son Fred P. Andresen who meticulously asks, "Did you mean to say this?" But, most important is the story from my dear dad, Arthur Andresen, who lived it and dug into his memory to tell me about it.

Contents

Foreword

This story takes place entirely in August, 1916. The year 1916 was one of the deadliest ever in world history. It was the end of empires and the empires did not want to go. The Kaiser attacked all of Europe. In France, the Battle of Verdun claimed one million lives and lasted ten months with no strategic result. The Battle of the Somme claimed fifty thousand British soldiers the first day, and a million and a half for both sides when it was over six months later. World War I also excited the inventive minds on all sides: The airplane, the dirigible, the tank, and poison gas killed men for the first time. London was bombed.

The Irish Easter Uprising cruelly turned the hearts of the Irish against their English overlords who shot civilians and executed prisoners. Russian Czar Nicolas II was about to lose his crown and his head, but never knew that he and his family's demise was only months away. Over the American border in Mexico, Pancho Villa, angered over President Wilson's support of Mexico's Carranza government, attacked the U.S. and General Pershing invaded Mexico with ten thousand men in pursuit, only to be beaten back after wandering in the desert, and, in the General's words "sneaking home under cover, like a whipped curr with its tail between its legs."

The United States was trying to keep its distance from it all, happily preoccupied with the first Coke, lots of jazz, and the opening of the San Diego Zoo with a female bear named Caesar. Boston was in ecstasy over the Red Sox winning the World Series; the pitcher, Babe Ruth. But the civil war on America's southern border refused to go away with the German Kaiser supplying guns to both sides through an El Paso hardware store. The infamous Zimmerman telegram exposed that farce which promised to return the American West to Mexico if they sided with Germany. It had just the opposite effect and sped America's entry into the war.

And oblivious to all this, two penniless immigrants, a Norwegian and an Irishman, meet in an El Paso bar and are lured to go to Mexico to fix a gold mine, ignoring all concerns for their safety and with parts, that they discover too late, purposely don't fit.

These two foreigners, erroneously called the Dos Gringos, had nothing in common and had totally different reasons for doing this, but they needed each other to stay alive and return to the relative safety of Texas. This is their mainly true and often entertaining story.

Chapter One

"Trust Me"

The bar doors banged open against the wall. Silhouetted in the afternoon sun was a man in a long coat, a derby on his head. The storm was over. He blinked as he bent and searched into the dark café. He took three steps, leaving the doors open. A boy ran to close them.

"Good afternoon, gentlemen," the silhouette announced.

At the bar were two foreigners who had just shaken hands for the first time. They glanced at the door. No one responded.

A tan-faced Norwegian, Arthur Johannesen, was on the first stool with his second beer. In his sweat-stained khakis and brown boots this bar-stop was only to catch his breath between the train station and the park where he planned to meet Pauline. Three stools to his left, sitting in front of the framed Budweiser poster of Custer's Last Stand was an Irishman, Michael Flaherty, a red-haired man in plaid pants and red suspenders, twirling a whiskey with his fingers.

"Welcome, *señor,* to the Rio Grande Café and Bar," said the Mexican bartender with his smiling teeth, curling mustache, and dirty apron.

In a corner a man strummed a guitar and sang in Spanish and a woman with a red rose in her hair danced, snapping her fingers, twirling her skirts, and showing her ankles. In another corner a man with a sweat-stained leather hat leaned into his girlfriend. At the far end of the bar was a fat man, his head dropped onto his chest as if in sleep.

In the mirror, Arthur watched the new man move to a table, remove his coat, brush it off, fold it into a rectangle, and lay it over a chair, smoothing it with the back of his hand and balancing his hat on top.

The Irishman turned to Arthur, "So you came from Tucson, did you? Is that far?"

"Ja, from Arizona. Long trip. Hot." He took another sip, smacked his lips and wiped his sandy mustache with his sleeve.

"You work there, did you?"

"In the mines, Morenci."

In the mirror, Arthur watched the new man as he smoothed the wrinkles off his pin-striped suit, positioned a chair at the table and sat down, brushing imaginary crumbs off the white table cloth.

"I am looking for a job," said Flaherty. "I'm from Ireland, I am."

Arthur did a double take. "No jobs in Ireland?"

"Oh yes, but big trouble, too," said Flaherty, "and other reasons."

Arthur's thought drifted for a moment. Why had he ever left Norway? He remembered the snow, the crunching whiteness, the disciplined but loving family life. It was predictable and sweet. Only for Pauline was he sitting in this hot bar in Texas.

"Do you serve meals here?" the new man shouted, looking around for a response.

Arthur thought the man showy—in his pin-striped suit, shouting for service.

"*Sí,* señor." The bartender called for the little boy, "Paco! *Pronto!*" waving his towel toward the seated man.

Paco jerked an apron off a wall-hook, grabbed a menu, and stumbled around the sleeping man at the end of the bar to serve the customer.

"Beer, señor?" the bartender called.

"I'll have a glass of sauterne, if you please."

"Is that whiskey, señor?"

"It's wine. Do you have wine?"

"Sorry, señor, we have beer, whiskey, gin, tequila—no wine."

"Pity. A gin, then, with ice. With a tall glass of water."

"Sorry, señor, we have no ice on Tuesday."

"Pity. Without ice, then."

He scanned the menu and shouted to Paco. "Fly specks. I'll have the fly specks."

"Fly specks, señor?" Paco looked dumbfounded. "Where

you see fly specks?"

"Right here on the menu," the man said. "I'll have fly specks. If you don't have fly specks, you should get them off the menu." He wheezed out a laugh at his own joke.

Paco and the bartender laughed and nodded like obedient children. "Fly specks, sí. Fly specks."

"The steak. Medium rare. Pink center. The potatoes and green beans. Salad." Leaning back in his chair and sticking his thumbs in his vest pockets, the man surveyed the room, looking at the three at the bar, the musicians, and the couple kissing in the dark far corner, the lover's progress hindered by the size of his hat.

Arthur fingered the few bills and coins in his pocket, knowing it was exactly nine dollars and forty-seven cents, his total wealth, and that had to cover the beers, the cost of a room, and some meal or treat with Pauline, even before a job was secured. Pauline was the reason for his being back in El Paso. He could not get her out of his mind and hoped to marry her—if he could find a job.

"My name is Ayles, Geoffrey Ayles," the new man announced to the room, loudly enough to be heard over the guitar. "That is Geoffrey with a 'G.'" He loosened his tie.

No one spoke. The lovers paused to look at the man and returned to each other.

"Welcome to the Rio Grande Café and Bar, Señor Ayles," the bartender offered as he moved out from the bar and placed the warm gin and water in front of the visitor. "You come on the tren?"

"Yesterday, from Pittsburgh, by way of St. Louis," he said as if he were the stationmaster announcing the train's arrival. The Norwegian and the Irishman contemplated their drinks, and out the tops of their eyes watched Ayles in the mirror through the shelves of clean glasses.

"I'm endeavoring to hire a couple of men…"

The Norwegian jerked up from studying his beer and the Irishman slammed down his glass. They turned and saw Paco serving the new man a plate of sliced tomatoes and greens.

Ayles poured the gin into the water. "…to go a little into Mexico on a special assignment," and he looked about as if he were addressing a classroom.

Arthur and Flaherty turned back to the bar.

"Good pay and expenses." Ayles took his knife and fork and began to cut up his lettuce and tomatoes. "For a few weeks of easy work for the right men." He put a fork full of salad into his mouth and said, "No danger, of course."

The two watched Ayles in the mirror, their fingers rotating their glasses. The man on the last stool was snoring, his head on the bar.

"I need an engineer, a mechanical engineer or machine repairman. If anyone here knows of someone, I would certainly like to be informed. I am staying at the Hotel Paso Del Norte. The name is Ayles, Geoffrey Ayles." The Easterner pulled his handkerchief from his suit pocket and ran its tip about the edge of his glass and then sipped his gin.

"Are you an engineer, Johnson?" asked Flaherty. "You don't look like a digger."

With his eyes on the mirrored image of Ayles, Arthur said, "Of course I am. I have a paper to show it." He gave a bothered glance to the Irishman and returned to the visitor lifting a fork of tomato to his mouth. "But," said Arthur, "I came here to see my woman."

Paco served the steak, a sizzling slab of meat an inch thick dripping red juice over both sides of the plate; the potatoes and green beans on another dish.

The two at the bar slowly turned to get a better look.

Ayles tucked a napkin into the top of his vest.

Arthur turned his head, hesitated, then asked, "Fixing what?"

"Repairing a mine's machinery," Ayles said, "Simple equipment, diesel engine, belts, crushing machine, that sort of thing."

"How long?

"Two weeks, maybe three at the longest." Ayles ran his thumb across the edge of his knife.

"Señores, look!" The bartender slapped a torn copy of *The El Paso Herald* on the bar, "Villa killed seventeen mining engineers. Lined them up and shot them."

Arthur glanced at the paper, then looked at the headlines a little closer and took another sip of beer. But the Norwegian and the Irishman were watching the steak and the man eating it.

"Dangerous place, ay, Johnson?" Flaherty asked.

"The name is Johan-nes-sen. It's Norwegian. Been here long, Flattery?"

"Two weeks."

"And no job yet?"

"I train horses."

Ayles gestured toward the empty chairs. "Why don't you two gentlemen join me, so we can talk?"

The Norwegian and Irishman left their stools and moved to Mr. Ayles' table. The lover in the corner pushed his hat back and made more progress. Only the guitar now strummed a soft ballad. The dancing girl had gone.

"Have you eaten?" Ayles asked.

Arthur shrugged and shook his head no. Flaherty said nothing.

"Waiter! The same for these two gentlemen."

Arthur stroked the stubble on his face. Flaherty rubbed his hands.

"Ayles, Geoffrey Ayles." He offered his hand. "With a 'G.'"

"Johannesen, Arthur."

"Michael Flaherty."

"What is your profession, gentlemen?" He took out a small pad and a pencil from his coat pocket.

Johannesen began, "Ja vell, I am machinist, journeyman machinist since age nineteen. I have document in my suitcase. In Norwegian." Arthur continued, "I am here to join my crew at the smelter. I was sent from the Phelps Dodge copper mines, to help with the smelting and refining operation here—ja, to get it set up and running."

Flaherty shot a look at Johannesen and flicked a smile, admiring the Norwegian's rapid advance from unemployed miner to construction crew leader.

Ayles laid down his pencil, leaned forward, spoke in a confidential voice, and looked into their eyes, "I represent J. J. Fulbright, president and owner, the Pittsburgh Mining Company, and we have a gold mine in Mexico a little ways over the border. It's broken down and needs a little repair." He watched their eyes as he took another bite of steak. "Only a temporary job," he added, "until the mine manager recovers from his illness."

The Irishman interrupted, "My colleague, Johnson here…" Arthur snapped a puzzled look at the Irishman who continued, "…that is right down his line, and we, together we can… What is the compensation for this highly qualified expertise, Mr. Ayles, understanding of course it is only for a short time." He rubbed his hands. "We would be missing our very good pay at our assignment at the Phelps Dodge Smelting and Refining Company."

Arthur looked away, then at the Irishman. Something told him not to interrupt. With no money for a ring to offer the woman he came to see, silence was the better option at this point.

The three talked about the mines in Morenci, the Revolution, until two steaks with the fresh tomato salads were served up by Paco, struggling under the tray.

Ayles leaned back with a confident smile, watching the

two consume their steaks.

While their mouths were bulging, Ayles offered, "You asked about the pay. It is $25 per week for each of you. Naturally, you will not want that paid in Mexico where it will be stolen. So it will be paid here when you return."

Arthur watched the easterner's eyes, flitting between his two candidates.

Flaherty halted a chunk of meat on the way to his overloaded mouth and mumbled, "Mr. Ayles, we do appreciate your consideration for the surety of our compensation, but the two of us will need to be paid half up front, here in El Paso, before we leave, sir."

Arthur raised his eyebrows, hesitated, then nodded in agreement.

Ayles folded his notes and returned them to his pocket. "I see you are wise men. Fair enough."

Arthur listened carefully, deciding to say nothing and continued to chew his steak.

"We will put that in a bank tomorrow morning," Ayles said. "Of course this in addition to expenses. I will advance you expense money, fifty dollars which will be enough for the assignment, but I will want an accounting, mind you," and he looked at Arthur for commitment.

"Within two weeks or so," said Ayles, "my representative or I will come to the mine, assess your progress, and settle accounts. You can then get paid the balance due in dollars or pesos. Is that acceptable?"

Flaherty answered for the newly formed team. "Fair, Mr.

Ayles."

"You'll be my guest tonight at the Paso Del Norte. But you'll have to share a room, I hope you don't mind. Economy, you see." He sipped his gin. "I'll arrange for you at The First National Bank at ten. We'll pick up some new parts at eleven o'clock sharp tomorrow; I'll give you full instructions, and put you on the train to Chihuahua."

"Chihuahua?" Arthur asked, "Where's Chihuahua, Mr. Ayles?"

"South." Ayles cocked his head toward Mexico. "Those mountains out there are Chihuahua. The train leaves at three. Is it firm then?"

"Firm, Mr. Ayles." Flaherty offered his hand.

"Agreed, Mr. Johannesen?"

"Ja," he hesitated. "OK, you bet," said Arthur and he shook Ayles' un-calloused hand. Arthur pulled a watch out of his pocket. "Ah, I'm late. Thanks for the dinner, Mr. Ayles." He laid some coins on the bar, grabbed his suitcase, replaced his hat and said, "I'll be at the hotel later," and raced for the door. Then he stopped. He rubbed his face and looked to the bartender.

"Sí, señor, I know what you need." He called the boy, "Paco, show the man the washroom. He is going to meet a señorita." And he winked at Arthur.

In the shed out back the Norwegian took a straight razor from his suitcase, soaped his face with a yellow bar hanging from a string, and over a bowl of cold water, scraped the stubble off his cheeks, leaving a small cut on his chin.

Chapter Two

The Promise

Arthur sprinted the four blocks to San Jacinto Plaza, the shady central square of El Paso with a fountain and a pond with three live alligators. On the four bordering streets, a few honking cars and horse-drawn wagons vied for space. Under the protecting elms and oaks, wooden benches circled the pond and lined the dirt paths leading to the four corners. Sparrows chirped their glee, the storm was over. Arthur took a deep breath and began his search for Pauline's trolley.

He swept off an empty bench with his hat and sat down facing the corner of Oregon and Main Streets as Pauline instructed in her letter. A young couple, holding hands, walked across the green. Near him, three old men sat on a bench, leather hats pulled over their faces, heads bowed in an afternoon siesta delayed by the storm. Arthur turned slowly and surveyed the surrounding streets, taking another peek at his pocket watch. It read 4:16.

Excited at seeing Pauline, he didn't give Norway another thought. He reviewed his last trip all in his mind: riding the trolley just to see her again; her smile, that smile on the second trolley trip which invited a response; his beating heart as he voiced that first hello on the third trolley trip; and after the fourth trip the talks she agreed to in the café and in the park. His heart was throbbing again, just like it was the first time that smile turned into a conversation, his with a Norwegian accent, her English better but still with that inflection typical to her immigrant roots in "German Texas" near San Antonio.

A trolley screeched to a halt on Oregon Street. Out of it stepped five people he couldn't make out against the afternoon sun. Two went down Oregon and two down Main, and one walked up the path directly toward him. She carried a wide brimmed hat with dangling ribbons. The sun's backlight outlined her slim figure under the folds of the white summer dress that danced just above her ankles. Her brown hair was done up in a bun with enticing strands falling on each side of her face. Arthur's heart pounded in his ears. He licked his lips. Pauline increased her pace, breaking into a run the last few steps, smiling, arms open. She embraced him with a kiss. Then holding him at arm's length she said, "Just as you said, Arthur. The Southern Pacific didn't let us down."

"Pauline!" He took off his hat and rotated its brim in his hands. "I'm so happy to see you again." She is really here, he thought, smiling, just as he dreamed; even better. Her eyes, a sparkling hazel green, spoke a hope and a promise. What beauty!

She pulled him back down to the bench. "Arthur. You must be tired."

"I wrote you, the mines closed down."

"That's not a problem." She ran her hand over his hair. "My father said he would find you a job here with the hardware company where he works."

"How's your mother?" he said, avoiding telling her his plans. "She was so sweet to me."

"She is fixing dinner soon. My father was away before. I have told him all about you. He is sometimes gone for weeks." She motioned with her hand toward the south. "Mom liked you because you cleaned your plate and had manners."

"That's a good reason. But I didn't know she would fix a dinner the first night."

Pauline laughed, leaned over, and kissed him. Then a longer kiss followed and she moved closer.

His eyes dropped shyly. "It's so nice to be with you, even for a short time."

Arthur looked around, getting a feel for a place he thought might well be a part of his new home, if all worked out as he hoped. It didn't have the charm of Norway, but it had Pauline.

"What do you mean 'short time?' You are coming to meet mother and father tonight, aren't you?"

"Well, I was about to tell you, there is a little change."

"Change? What could change, Arthur? We are expecting you. Father is leaving again tomorrow." She straightened.

He quickly added, "Already I found a job."

She raised her eyebrows. "What? So soon?"

"This was unexpected, but it will take only few weeks, maybe less. The pay is good. And then I will talk to your father. When I meet him, I want to ask for your hand in marriage, and have the ring in my pocket."

"But, Arthur—." She backed off.

"I know. I'll meet your father when I return. I'll be ready for him then."

"But, Arthur—."

"It's important. I have to do this my way, Pauline. I have to earn you myself."

She moved back to him. "What is it?" she said. "What is this so-important job?"

"A supervisory job to fix a gold mine." His eyes wandered.

"Here in El Paso?"

"No, in Mexico."

"*Mexico?*" Pauline stuttered. "You are not serious. Don't you know about the murders, the fighting there?"

"It's a simple job."

"But, dear Arthur, you came here to see *me*, and to meet my family." She was confused and inside felt like a shock of some kind. "This is *not* good news."

He felt her voice turn cold and saw her glance back toward the trolley stop.

"Oh, Pauline. Please trust me. I love you so much." He pulled her close, ran his hands about her back. She folded into him and her leg came up on him as far as the long dress and public display would allow.

"I don't want you to go. Please stay here. Say no to this thing, Arthur. There are plenty of jobs right here."

He buried his head in her neck, inhaling her sweet scent but saying nothing, wrestling with his pride of authority in this affair and his desire to stay in her arms. He began to have second thoughts; but no, make the money, buy the ring, that is the way to do this.

"When do you leave?" she asked, pushing him off and looking into his eyes for a deeper truth, a real commitment.

"Tomorrow. The man gave us a room in the Del Norte hotel tonight."

"*Us?* Who are *us?*" She backed off again.

"My crew. Well, only one, an Irishman. His name is Flattery or something like that."

"An Irishman! Where did you find an Irishman? This is not what I expected, Arthur." She lowered her head. "People are being killed there. I'm afraid for you."

"It's not my war."

"But Arthur, I promised my parents I'd bring you home to meet them. All my father has seen of you are the few pictures. What will I tell him? You know how fathers are. They want to shake your hand, look you in the eyes, ask questions."

"It is only for a few weeks. It will be easy and the money is good."

"Who is this Irishman?" she asked.

"I just met him…he says he is good with horses…I almost walked away, Pauline. But something told me I could use someone to talk to—he may even help. Two more hands."

Pauline shook her head and lifted his calloused hands. "Arthur, I am disappointed. You know that. But, you're going to do what you're going to do." Then she reached into her purse. "You said some very sweet things to me last time you were here, Arthur, and in your letters. It was so sweet." She pulled him closer and looked into his eyes. "I meant what I said then. Money is not important. I love you for who you are. This is for you." She opened his hand and placed a heart shaped gold locket in his palm.

Arthur pushed the button with his thumb, and it snapped opened to a picture of Pauline's smiling face. Wordless, Arthur shook his head, and felt a twisting inside. "I, I can't believe this." He pulled her to him and kissed her with a growing doubt he was doing the right thing to go to Mexico. He rubbed the gold case. "I will keep this next to me, right here." He patted his heart. "But, Pauline," he apologized, "I have nothing for you. I told you I will work hard and I will tell you again. I love you so much. I will be back very soon and then we can…" he looked at the picture again, "…you know. We had such sweet times before." His words came slowly, but he looked into her hazel eyes and said, "I promise." He kissed the locket and slipped it into his shirt pocket next to the letter.

"I will wait, Arthur, as I have already for three long months. I don't know," and she flashed her eyes and shook her head, "the señoritas are very pretty down there. I will wait—two more weeks." She held up two fingers. "Just come back. I have your word?"

He saw the tears in her eyes. "I promise. You bet. Señoritas mean nothing to me," he said. "You must be hungry," he added. "I am not fit to meet your parents anyway. Would you like to eat?"

"That's all right," she said. "I must head home to tell mother you are not coming tonight."

"I'm sorry." His eyes lowered.

He mumbled something in Norwegian, then looked both ways and pulled her toward him and kissed her long and hard.

Passing children snickered, covering their mouths, making big eyes and kissy faces.

"Your mustache tickles," Pauline giggled. "I love it. And when you say 'I promise. You bet,' that is truth to me, I feel happy. That will be my 'locket' until you return."

Chapter Three

Pride

otel Paso Del Norte, a nine-story double building of red and white brick, was the finest in this border town. Room 314 had two beds, a sink, and the smell of tobacco smoke. It faced the back alley with a view through clean windows of the weathered backsides of adjacent buildings. Arthur sat on his bed and ran his hand over the cool clean sheets and wondered what Pauline would be like in bed. He hoped she would be proud of him.

"Johannesen," said Flaherty, sitting on the other bed, "we don't have to do this, you know."

Arthur bent his head, skeptical, examining Flaherty out the tops of his eyes, and wondered who this Irishman really was. "How's that?" Arthur said, wondering why his roommate was saying this now, after their commitment?

"If it is so dangerous," Flaherty said, "as they all say, why do it?"

Arthur puzzled. Do I need this man? This should be a

quick job—not far away. But I'm a fool to go alone. Maybe he's right?

"We shook hands, Flattery, both of us."

"But we haven't taken the money yet. What do you say?"

"Are you a quitter?" Arthur asked.

"I don't quit what I start, but we haven't started yet."

"If we take the money and go to Mexico tomorrow, that is starting," Arthur said and squinted his eyes as if he could then better see into this Irishman who would be his partner. "We have to trust each other," said Arthur. "You can't run out on me if things get tough."

Flaherty did not respond. Arthur, dusted off and folded his jacket and laid his hat on top. "Ja, vell, do you want to back out?"

"Do *you*?" Flaherty asked.

"I want to buy a ring for Pauline, my girlfriend," and he pointed in the direction of the park. "She is my only interest." Arthur sat on the bed and looked Flaherty in the eyes. "I shook hands on the Mexico deal. She says her father will get me a job. I don't need her father for the ring. I can earn the money myself. But then I will return and maybe take her father's job with pride. I am not a beggar."

"For a little money, that's right," the Irishman said. "I have nowhere else to go, if truth be known. You have a girlfriend. That's good. I just need time," he paused, "to find myself."

Arthur slipped off his boots, not wanting to dig further

into his roommate's mind. "She is a jewel. I don't want to mess things up."

Flaherty shook his head, "Lucky man you are."

"I know your problem. I don't trust that man Ayles," Arthur said. "His hands are too white. We'll get our hands dirty, Flattery. Be sure you're ready. This is not a one-man job."

The Irishman nodded in resignation.

"We'll get the job done—two or three days," said Arthur, "get paid and get back, ja? It won't even take two weeks I think. But I don't know what a horseman is going to do."

"You can never tell, Johannesen. There're a lot of horses in Mexico."

"Let's see how it goes in the morning, ja? We can always back out if he doesn't deliver on the parts, the money, or for any other reason. But for now, Flattery, we go to sleep, ja?"

"The name is Fla-her-ty."

"Ja, Fla-her-ty. "

Chapter Four

The Man in Black

In their sweat-stained shirts and pants, the Norwegian and the Irishman pushed out of the heavy bronze doors of The First National Bank at ten forty-five, with smiles on their faces and twenty-five dollars each in the bank. Arthur pulled a small pad from his pocket and scribbled a note to record the event.

Ayles smiled, again in his freshly brushed three-piece pin-striped suit and derby. They walked five blocks to a three-storied brick building standing alone by two sets of railroad tracks, one set along the loading dock long enough for three freight cars. On the building's side, in two-foot letters, was written KRAKAUER, ZORK, AND MOYE, WHOLESALE HARDWARE, MACHINERY AND SUPPLIES. They climbed up onto the loading platform. It had the dusty smell of a warehouse and the busy sounds of creaking carts and shouting men. Zork, as everyone called it, was the largest hardware distributor in the Rio Grande

Valley, founded some years before by three Jewish merchants from the German part of Texas near San Antonio. El Paso del Norte, as the Spanish named this city in the seventeenth century, was a historic gateway, a pass north through the southern end of the Rockies. Zork was the source for everything, to both sides of the United States and Mexican border—and to anyone who would pay up-front in dollars, increasingly in short supply in Mexico.

"The waitress at the hotel," Arthur pointed back toward the Del Norte. "She said there was lots of fighting close to here."

"I have it on better advice, gentlemen," Ayles said. "The news just this morning is that the Federáles, the government troops, safely hold the northern parts of Mexico, where you are going."

"And, Pancho? What's his name?" Flaherty asked, "What about him? He is everywhere the waitress said. He killed the engineers, she said. Villa controls Chihuahua, she said."

"Waitress? What does a waitress know?" said Ayles. "You won't be there long enough to worry about that bandit. Trust me." Ayles turned to a clerk.

Arthur pointed to a stack of wooden crates. "Are these the parts for the mine, Ayles?"

The clerk, in horn-rimmed glasses and a blue and white striped apron, patted one of the crates. "The supplies, Mr. Ayles, everything you will need according to your list." The crates were marked "Agricultural Implements." The clerk removed a hand written four-page packing list from his clipboard and handed it to Arthur.

Arthur looked it over and said, "Mr. Ayles, what exactly are we supposed to do? You said you tell us details today."

"It's straight forward for experts like you. The mine belongs to the owner in Pittsburgh, Mr—."

"Ja, I remember, Fulbright," Arthur said.

"Yes," Ayles continued, "Fulbright. The mine has been producing high-grade gold ore for three years. The machinery needs repair." He patted one of the boxes. This equipment is what the mining engineers have determined is needed."

Arthur raised his hand. "Wait a minute," he said. "What exactly needs to be fixed? Who ordered these parts?"

"The previous manager," Ayles said, "made up this list before he left. He was a competent man, like you. Trust me."

The shipping clerk handed Arthur a pencil. "I understand you are the leader of this team, Mr. Johannesen," the clerk said. "If you will please inspect this list and see what is there and if you lack anything."

Arthur took the list, scanned it quickly, saw listed familiar part names. Arthur knew he had to trust what was ordered by the former engineer. He had confidence in his own ability to improvise, if necessary. "My assistant here," Arthur said, "he will check it off." He handed the list to Flaherty.

Flaherty read down the list, but stumbled over part names like "torque rods, reduction gears, main bearings, extension shafts," confirming to Arthur his assistant hadn't a clue what it was all about.

Arthur, when Flaherty was finished, said, "I didn't hear any tools listed. Put down these: Crescent wrenches; ten, fifteen, eighteen inches; Stillson wrenches four and six inches; a twentyfour-inch chain wrench."

Ayles interrupted, "Mr. Johannesen, I understand there are tools at the site, we sent them last year. We have to watch expense, you know."

"Tools are gone now, Mr. Ayles," Arthur said. "Ja, you can bet on that. I don't go without my own tools." Arthur continued, "Heavy ball-peen hammer, maybe forty ounces; two pry bars, complete set of screwdrivers, quarter and half inches." Arthur continued, "Kerosene torches, two sledgehammers, two crow bars, and don't forget emery cloth—and lots of rags. And big cans of grease and oil."

The clerk scribbled away.

"Mr. Ayles," Flaherty asked, "are you sure now you don't want to come with us to ascertain the accuracy of the engineer's estimates?"

Ayles turned away, pretending not to hear. "You have a good Mexican crew waiting for you. This envelope has all the plans of the mine and its machinery. In addition, how to get from the train to the mine is written in English and Spanish." Flaherty took the envelope, opened it and began to read. It was clear Ayles was prepared for his new crew.

Arthur walked away. At the far end of the loading platform he noticed more wooden crates also marked

"Agricultural Implements." Checking off a list was a tall thin man in a homburg and a black suit with a pointed white handkerchief in the breast pocket. The man was pointing and giving orders in fluent Spanish, but with an accent Arthur could not identify. Arthur leaned against a pole, his thumbs in his belt, and watched as the man's crates were loaded onto a truck. The black-suited man turned and noticed Arthur watching him and held his eyes directly on Arthur, as if studying him for later reference. Arthur turned away and returned to where Flaherty was bending over a crate with Ayles, tracing something with his finger on an opened map.

"All the tools you requested will be packed in a moment," confirmed the clerk with the clipboard. "There are now ten crates total." Ayles waived his hand and the shipment was loaded into a red Reo truck, ready to grind away toward Juarez, across the Rio Grande into Mexico.

"Ayles," Arthur asked, "who is that man?" And he nodded his head down the platform to where the man in the black suit had stood.

"What man?" said Ayles.

The platform was empty. There was no one there.

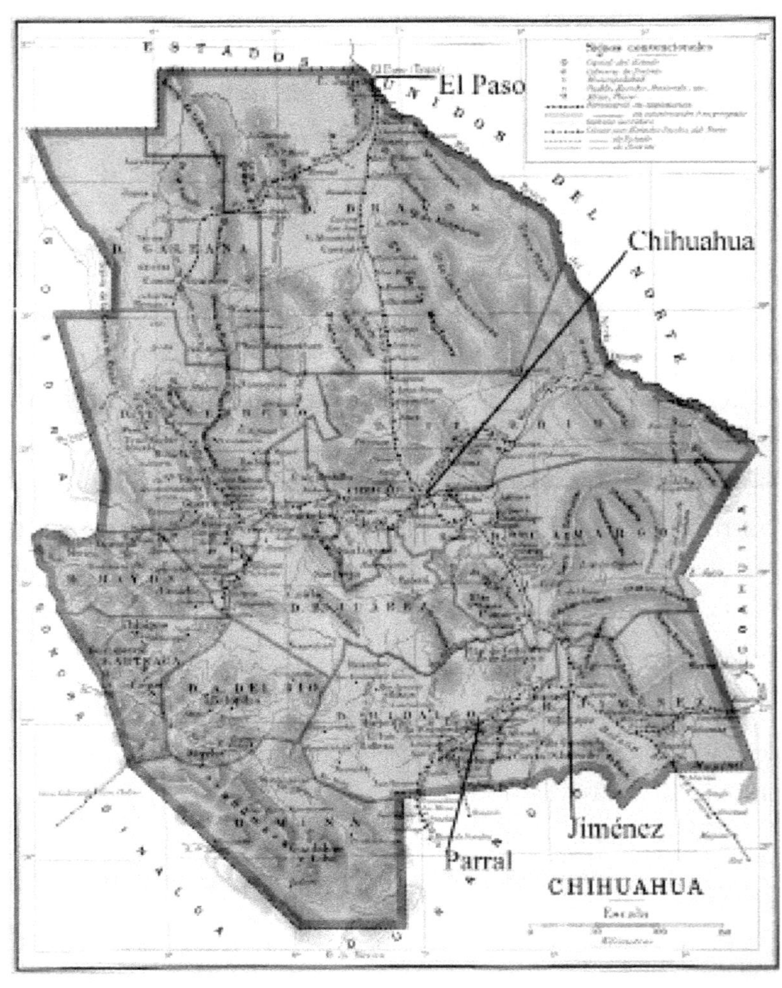

Map of Chihuahua, Mexico adapted from Reseña geográfica y estadística. Paris: Libreria de la Vda. de C. Bouret, 1909.

Chapter Five
Crossing the River

The three men, Ayles, Arthur and Flaherty, climbed into a black Ford Model-T Sedan with a driver. Following the red truck, the car belched and chugged toward the bridge across the Rio Grande with the Norwegian and the Irishman in the back seat with their luggage on their laps. The American border guards and customs agents stopped the truck, studied the packing lists and waved them on. The river was only a muddy sliver where forty feet below, Mexican boys in the knee-deep water called for pedestrians to throw them coins.

Juarez was a maze of adobe buildings and narrow streets filled with people, burros, and a few cars honking their way through the traffic. Deposited on the street side of the Juarez train station, the three men faced a decaying stucco building not much larger than the Hotel Paso Del Norte lobby. Out of horse-drawn wagons and on foot, passengers wrestled bundles and cases toward the trains. The three men muscled through a milling wall of people with bulging bags, strapped suitcases, and caged chickens, and who were all at once calling out to their relatives or friends. The place smelled of sweat and tobacco smoke. The Reo truck arrived at the end of the wooden platform and the crates were unloaded under the eyes of the clerk from Zork's.

"I will try, Mr. Ayles, sir," said the clerk, "to get these loaded into the first car if possible."

"Do you have the tickets?" Ayles asked.

The clerk pulled an envelope from an apron pocket and gave it to Ayles.

Leaning on a pole and on each other was a squad of swarthy men, smoking, in dirty white uniforms criss-crossed with bandoleers of ammunition for their long rifles. A bayonet and small cloth pouches were attached to their belts. They wore mustaches and little caps with big badges, and looked half asleep. This was the first look the foreigners had of the Federales, the side in the war trying to hold power.

"This is our train, is it?" Flaherty asked.

There were twelve cars and no engine. The clerk handed some cash to a foreman and the crates were lifted into the first freight car.

"There you are, sir," the clerk reported.

"Good job, Ernest." Ayles handed the clerk some coins.

The doors of the second freight car stood open and out stepped the black-suited man with his homburg and white kerchief. Arthur straightened and watched him out the corner of his eye. "Mr. Ayles," said Arthur, "that's the man who was on the Zork's platform with us."

The black-suited man watched the heavy doors slide shut and padlocked and pocketed the key. Without a glance to the three foreigners, the man walked toward the first-class passenger car and climbed on board.

"Just another businessman," Ayles said, "Not important."

"You said you would come check on us in two weeks, Mr. Ayles," Flaherty reminded.

"You can count on it, my friends. You should be finished by then."

"Ja, I hope so. I have other things to do," said Arthur and he glanced back toward El Paso.

"By the way," Ayles added, "the mine has a name, *La Promesa*."

"How far is this trip to La Promesa?" Flaherty asked.

"A couple of days," Ayles said.

On the sides of the cars were the words in faded gold, *Ferrocarril Nacional de Mexico*.

"A couple of *days*?" said Arthur. "You said the mine was just over the border."

"I said Chihuahua was across the border, gentleman. You are standing in it now. This is a big state, half the size of France, and the mine is in the south part. This train will stop in Chihuahua City, then in a town called Jiménez, where you will transfer to a mountain train to Parral. It's all on the map I gave you." He handed the Irishman an envelope. "Here's your expense money in pesos. The rate is ten cents per peso today. Guard it carefully. Keep it on your body. Good luck, gentlemen." Ayles gave a quick smile. "And here are your tickets. *Bon voyage.*"

A steaming engine backed onto the train with a crash and coupled up, shaking the lounging soldiers.

"Mr. Ayles," Flaherty said, as he grabbed the railing by the car's door, "what is the mill manager's name, in case he comes back?"

Ayles hesitated, his eyes searching the sky. "Abercrombie, Rufus Abercrombie. I doubt if you will be meeting him."

Looking at their tickets, Arthur and Flaherty pushed past sweating families waving at relatives and slipped into car number five. Ayles turned and disappeared into the crowd.

Arthur put his suitcase next to Flaherty's in the overhead rack. The door clanked shut with a sound of finality. The train jerked, and Arthur grabbed a railing on the back of the seat. It jerked two or three times in the same direction, which he saw, bending to look out the dirty windows, signaled they were under way south, away from El Paso.

They looked around at the people, the chickens, and at each other. Flaherty muttered, "Holy Mother of God!"

"We said we would think it over," Arthur said, "but we didn't. Ayles did everything he said he would do." Out of his shirt pocket Arthur pulled the small gold locket, opened it and looked at Pauline's smiling face and whispered to himself, "It's for the ring." But he also thought the offer from her father now seemed more acceptable. But it was too late.

On the Juarez station platform, Geoffrey Ayles faded into the crowd of departing well-wishers, men and women with their bundles and babies, now that the only train to Chihuahua was on its way. He turned and watched it leave the Juarez station, the caboose pursued by a racing trainman who jumped onto the back stairs just as it left the station platform. The gentleman from Pittsburgh reexamined his feelings, now that his job was done.

He'd hired two good men, he thought, not knowing anything about their ability to do the job they were hired for, but he knew it really wouldn't matter. A self-confident Norwegian and an eager Irishman; maybe the last two desperate foreigners in El Paso who would take a job like that. It had been over two weeks now, the ads in the paper bringing nothing, and the visits to the other bars producing blank stares or laughs at the ludicrous offer to go to Mexico and fix a mine. Most likely the Norwegian could fix it, but he knew not with the parts packed in those cases.

He didn't want to go to the mine again, Ayles thought, not like the last time, the unfortunate Abercrombie affair. Maybe they will keep each other out of trouble, or make it doubly worse. It was not in his hands, now. Good men, those two. He'd done his job.

The train's receding whistle still drifted across the adobe walls of Cuidad Juarez. The relatives were gone home or to shop at the street vendors. But, there was the wall, the wall ten steps away where Ayles watched the executions only weeks before when the Federales rounded up three Villistas, stood them against it, and he found himself in a small group of silent witnesses to the killing of the three men. Just like that. In the middle of the day. The victims looked like fathers and brothers, and the look of disbelief on their faces as rifles fired and the wall behind them shattered, spraying dust from the bullets that had gone through their bodies. One at a time they died, the soldiers having to reload. Walking to that wall now, with his fingers he felt into the bullet holes. He felt conflicted, wishing he could somehow send a blessing of protection for his two hired men on the train heading south, but maybe, with two of them, it wouldn't work out like the last time.

He walked away, toward his waiting black Model-T and the safety of El Paso and his room, a deluxe room, in the Hotel Paso del Norte, to have a drink of gin and wait for news.

Chapter Six
Roast Beef and Green Chilies

"What did she say?" Arthur asked about Flaherty's conversation with the nuns across the aisle.

"They sort of speak English," said Flaherty.

"I can't hear. The chickens — too loud."

"She said it won't take two days." Flaherty brushed away flies. "We will be in Chihuahua in the morning—if we are not stopped that is."

"Why stopped?" Arthur sat by the window and Flaherty on the aisle, across from the nuns.

"Banditos," Flaherty said. "But maybe not this time because of the soldiers on board, she said, and the important people in First Class." He thought a moment and added, "Or maybe she said they might stop us *because* of the important people in First Class. She has an accent, not always easy."

"Ja, thanks." Arthur turned to the window again. The sun was a ball of orange on the western horizon, the desert sky aflame under long strings of golden and gray clouds. He was getting used to the Southwestern deserts and mountains: Texas, Arizona. When he became absorbed in the western sunsets, he didn't miss Norway so much. There the sun never set in the summer and never rose in the winter and everything was predictable. Even through the dirty train window the vastness, the sunsets, were a sight to be remembered. There was the rhythmic clicking of the rails underneath and the steady puffing of the engine ahead. For Arthur it almost made up for the crying children, the squawking chickens, the shouting men at their card game, and the hot smells of cigarettes, chilies, and sweat.

"We are being treated by these generous servants of God," the Irishman said, nodding toward the nuns. Flaherty had a large slice of bread in his hand with a larger slice of beef and a green chili that hung off the end. Under their black habits, the two young nuns were smiling at the foreigners.

Arthur leaned forward, nodded and smiled. The nuns handed out another serving of bread, beef, and chili across the aisle. The meat was still warm. Arthur and Flaherty had not eaten since their breakfast at the hotel. They stuffed the meat in their mouths and filed the chilies into the seat pockets ahead. "For future reference," Arthur said.

"The one with all the eyebrows," said Flaherty, "is Sister Elizabeth and the one with the big smile and the roast on her lap is Sister Mercedes. They both speak some English. Very nice don't you think, Johannesen?"

Sisters Mercedes and Elizabeth were giggling with their hands over their mouths, glancing at the Irishman's plaid pants and bush of red hair and how he would raise his eyebrows when he spoke to them.

Arthur took a bite of the beef, leaned forward and smiled his thank you to the nuns. The juicy roast rested on the nun's lap, unwrapped in heavy stained paper. Sister Mercedes held a big knife and licked her fingers. Sister Elizabeth handed slices of the meat to the mother and children on the seats ahead of them.

"What do we do for a drink?" asked Arthur licking his lips.

"A man will come through, they said."

"Let's hope so."

The conductor, short, and with sweat rings under his arms the size of dinner plates, squeezed his overhanging belly through the doorway and ordered something with a high pitched voice as if commanding troops. "Sister Elizabeth says he wants all the shades down so nobody can see in. Safety measure she says."

"But no drinks, eh?"

The seats, old and soft, were covered in a floral patterned fabric. The sounds died down. The babies and the chickens went to sleep. The lights were dimmed. A man behind started to snore with puffing sounds like those of the engine ahead. The two foreigners also dozed off—until the engineer hit the brakes.

Suitcases, caged chickens, and half the sleeping passengers, including the nuns with the roast beef, were thrown onto the floor. Arthur struggled back onto his seat and lifted the window shade. "Men, guns, horses," he exclaimed. "Something burning ahead."

Long blasts poured from the train's whistle. "Soldiers now running around," Arthur said, wiping the window with his sleeve and squinting into the dark. "They're shooting." The train jerked and started to back up. Soon it screeched to a halt and they all fell the other way. "The soldiers back on the train now," Arthur reported. The train jerked forward and gained speed. Then there was a jolt and crash and out the window he saw burning timbers tumbling through the air as the engine, with its big "cow catcher" on the front, cleared the tracks of the burning wood.

Arthur leaned over and smiled at the nuns who were both crowded at their window, their faces plastered to the glass, the roast beef on the floor.

When Arthur awoke, Flaherty was bent over the seat-back table, reading the instructions from Ayles. The sun was well above the horizon. "We'll be in Chihuahua city soon," Flaherty said. The nuns were asleep. At last Flaherty opened the bag of food from Ayles. It was wrinkled bread, cold roast beef, and two warm bottles of beer.

Soon the train slowed and crept into the station. They saw little on the passing dirt streets of early-morning Ciudad Chihuahua—a dusty town with a few street vendors, horses, wagons—and soldiers. As soon as the train squealed to a stop, Arthur jumped onto the platform and ran to keep watch on the freight car. It was opened to unload some cases, and he watched until it was locked again and the conductor called the departure.

The new conductor was a tall stick of a man with over-sized pants hanging from leather braces. He called out they were going to Jiménez, Torreon, Zacatecas, San Luis Potosí, and Ciudad de México. The train jolted as a new car was added up front with soldiers and machine guns. Two soldiers boarded each car.

"How far to Jiménez, Flaherty?"

"The sisters say three hours. They get off there, too." He patted the map.

Sister Elizabeth leaned forward in her seat. "Are you going further, señores?"

Arthur answered. "We are going to repair a mine." He touched the map in Flaherty's hands. "Hidalgo del Parral. It is a safe place we were told."

"Oh," said Sister Mercedes with a scowl, "please be careful. We have heard some terrible things. Villa's most dangerous man, The Hawk, he is in those parts, señores."

"We have a contract," Arthur said. "We don't back out now." He shot a glance to Flaherty.

"That's right," Flaherty said with a hint of uncertainty. "We have a commitment, we do."

Out the windows the passing sights were becoming common: houses and chickens, women and children walking on the roads, cactus, palms, rocks, soldiers in trucks, rugged hills

In a cloud of whistling steam, the train screeched to a halt in the Jiménez station. Arthur and Flaherty hurried to arrange for the unloading as they were told the train would depart within twenty minutes. Sisters Elizabeth and Mercedes gathered their baskets and bid the foreigners goodbye. "Señores, we live here in the Convent of the Blessed Virgin." The sisters crossed themselves. "God bless and be careful."

No one was there to help. It was past two in the afternoon and Flaherty's schedule showed the train to Parral leaving at three. Flaherty called over some boys, waving a dollar bill, and with hand signals hired a long wagon with iron wheels and they struggled with the crates and got them alongside the track for Parral. But there was no train.

Flaherty asked around, shrugged his shoulders and said, "No one seems to know when the train will come. *Mañana*, they say. Maybe morning."

"We must guard the equipment," Arthur said. "Take turns, even if we have to stay up all night."

A man in a black suit with a gold watch chain walked up. The stationmaster was more helpful than they expected, offering to have the wagon locked in a freight shed for the night.

"I will pay the man five pesos now," Flaherty said, "and tomorrow five when we leave. He said to go to the hotel there," and he pointed to the crooked sign that read "Hotel

Paris" in fancy script on broken boards. They laughed and dragged their suitcases into the adobe building for the night. They didn't wander from the hotel, but Flaherty checked on the train schedule until eight when all was closed. They played checkers in the bar to pass the time. Arthur was the white checkers, Flaherty the red. Arthur won the first game and was winning the second when Flaherty asked a question. "Norway's a quiet and peaceful place. Why are you here?"

That was not a question Arthur wanted to confess to anyone, but he would try. "Why I am in America is hard to tell. Why I am in Mexico you already know."

"Why did you leave Norway?"

"I made a mistake." He moved his king forward. "Your turn."

Flaherty moved his piece away from Arthur's king.

"Sonya was a beautiful girl. We dated for years. Family friends. Talked about marriage, family, all those things. I had a good job—in my uncle Sven's diesel plant." Arthur looked at the checkerboard. "Ja vell, my move." He moved a piece out of the back row.

Flaherty jumped two whites into the back row and made himself a king. Arthur frowned.

"Then Ingrid, my friend Jurgen's pretty cousin came from Denmark. She took a liking to me. We went sailing on the Oslofjord one quiet evening. A small boat, centerboard. A big wind came up sudden like. We call them white squalls, ja, rough. She was next to me and before we knew it the boat capsized. We weren't far from the dock. Ingrid thought it all a big adventure. Ha! We swam and we neared the dock, there she was, Sonya, her hands on her hips, her skirt blowing in the wind. She walked away. I tried to see her again, but no, she wouldn't. I made a mistake. I loved Sonya. I planned a family in Norway. I promised her. Ingrid was just a boat ride, nothing serious. And here I am in broken down Hotel Paris playing checkers with you."

"Not your fault."

"I broke the trust. I trust myself with machines. Machines are predictable. I must learn to trust myself with women. I gave my word. It was my fault. I can't let that happen again."

"I know," said Flaherty. "When it comes to love, secrets don't keep."

"Ja vell, you win." Arthur said and lined up his checkers. "And what about you, Flaherty? You didn't really come to train horses did you?"

"No, you're right. It's hard for me to tell about it. Maybe later."

Arthur respected that, knowing it might be an unhappy story. He was sleepy in any case. They shared a bed, a mattress that hung like a hammock, sleeping in their clothes, lying back to back if for no other reason than to avoid the smell of the other's breath.

Chapter Seven

"76"

The day was already hot. Morning sunlight slanted through the grimy windows of El Café Feliz and onto the tables where men in railway uniforms were eating their breakfasts.

"Look at the tall man with the round hat," Flaherty said.

"He's the boss," said Arthur. "You can always tell the boss by the keys on his belt." The man's pressed blue uniform looked out of place in a dusty town in the middle of a revolution. "Look at the gold ropes on his collar," said Arthur. "He must be the boss, or a colonel or something."

On the man's head sat a short tube of a hat with a gold badge. His waxed mustache extended two inches beyond his cheeks, curling into circles. The other men wore gray and white bib overalls with matching caps and red bandanas around their necks. Breakfast was shredded pork with chili, black beans, and rice.

Confirming the Parral train was ready, the stationmaster opened the shed. Arthur pushed on the crates, checking to see if they had been opened. "Looks okay," Arthur said and wrote a note in his little book. "Pay the man his pesos," he said to Flaherty. The crates were loaded onto a flat car with wooden stakes.

"Look at this machine, Flaherty," Arthur said. The train had three passenger cars. The engine hissed steam as if alive, like a giant horse straining to go.

"Let's get on board," said Flaherty, pulling himself up the car's steps by the polished brass rods at the door.

"But look at this," Arthur insisted. The Norwegian liked anything mechanical and this was to him a piece of mechanical art. "Every part of the engine is shining black or shining brass." Over the dinner-plate sized headlight hung a big brass bell. The smokestack, tall as the engine itself, had a glistening brass ring around its top. The side of the cab was emblazoned with a large "76" in artistic gold and silver script.

"Come on, Johannesen," shouted Flaherty from the center car.

The man with the pressed blue suit and mustache stood by the first car, swinging his key ring and blowing his whistle. He looked up and down the track, and shouted, *"Todos Aborrrrrdos!"*

Arthur hurried into the car and lifted his suitcase onto the overhead rack of brass rods. In the otherwise empty car sat a family of seven: mother, father, children small and large, and a smiling grandmother with no teeth. Arthur looked around, smiled back, and nodded a greeting.

The engine puffed out of Jiménez, and after crossing a long bridge ground along cultivated fields with goats that gave the train a glance as it passed. The door into the first car opened. It was the conductor with a smile to match his mustache. He took the family's tickets and punched each one so the children could watch. He patted the children and joked with the grandmother. Turning to Flaherty and Arthur, he motioned with his hands. "Welcome to the *Express de Hidalgo del Parral*, señores. *Conductór Rodríquez, a sus ordenes.*" He saluted. "We don't see many Americanos these days."

"My partner and me here," Flaherty motioned to Arthur with his hand, "we are on an assignment."

The conductor took their tickets and punched them.

"Your engine," Arthur said. "It's a beautiful machine."

"Thank you, señor. The pride of Mexico. Even in these times, we keep it in perfect condition, and don't ask too much of it. It's as old as I am."

The conductor bent over and looked out the window. "We will be entering the canyon soon. Don't miss it." He turned to leave, then turned back. "Will you be coming back soon, señores?"

"About two weeks," Flaherty said.

The train was slowing and puffing harder. Arthur moved to the seat behind and slid open the window. The engine pulled and puffed, inching through the bare brown hills and over dry stream beds deepened by seasons of rain . The next window opened and Flaherty leaned out, sniffing the air as the breeze curled the heavy smoke onto the other side of the cars. Tall-eared jackrabbits bounced along and away from the noise. As the train snaked up the track, they could see both the engine and the red caboose. The sounds of the engine and the rhythmic clicking of the rails was an entrancing music.

"You like music, Flaherty?" Arthur asked.

Flaherty nodded. "What Irishman doesn't like music?"

"I know, you dance jigs—things like that. I mean…" and Arthur patted his heart. "Uncle Knut was, maybe still is, conductor of the Oslo orchestra. I miss that."

"I know what you mean, my friend. It all touches the heart, it does. You have a favorite?"

"Bach. I always like Bach. It's represents a beautiful order to me," said Arthur. "Everything in its right place."

"Yeah, me too. I can always count on Bach."

"I remember the guitar player in the bar," Arthur said. "It was only two days ago. After the dancing, it was a quiet song. Not Bach, but very pretty."

"Just two days," said Flaherty, thinking. "It feels like two weeks already. And here we are."

The hillsides steepened, enveloping the train and its track. The air smelled of fresh scrub and pine. Around a curve they approached a road where they were greeted by about thirty men, hauled up, turning, and struggling to control their frightened horses. "What's this?" said Arthur.

They were tall men, with wide sombreros, on big horses, and each had two or three rifles, pistols, and bullet-belts criss-crossing their chests. Several fired into the air, like it was accidental. Arthur and Flaherty pulled in their heads and ducked between the seats, bullets flew through the open window where their heads had been and crashed through others, lodging in the wall over the cowering children.

"Bandidos," Arthur said as the train entered a narrow canyon and the smoke swirled about. They slammed the windows shut. The conductor opened the door and called in, "Everyone safe?"

Frightened faces said, "Yes."

"Just in time, amigos. If we were minute later, they would stop and rob us all. Twice last month."

Chapter Eight
"Viva Villa"

Like a triumphant stallion, the shining engine proudly marched into the station at Hidalgo del Parral and engulfed the happy greeters in a cloud of hissing steam. Next to the platform stood a long wagon and two tired-looking horses, one a sorrel and the other a motley white, their noses tucked into feedbags. A whiskered old man under a sweat-stained leather sombrero sat in the driver's seat with a whip in his hand.

Letting the family exit first, the two foreigners stepped onto the platform and saw before them a city of weathered baroque churches and grand colonial buildings. The city still reflected its Spanish regal past of elegant buildings, churches, parks and fountains it enjoyed since the sixteenth century. Neither of the Europeans had ever seen anything like it.

"Señores from Señor Ayles? El Paso?" a voice called. A boy was waving his hand. He was about fifteen and wore white trousers that no longer reached his ankles and a tunic top gathered at the waist by a rope. His black hair hung from under a leather hat with a wavy brim, and he carried a rifle as long as he was tall.

"We are from Señor Ayles." Flaherty raised his hand.

"*Sigame por favor*," the boy said, waving them to follow. He slung the rifle over his shoulder, turned, and walked through the onlookers to the wagon with his head held high.

"Are you from the mine called *La Promesa*?" Arthur, sprinting to catch up, asked the boy.

"*Si, La Promesa*. We take you *La Promesa, por las instrucciones del* Señor Ayles," the boy answered.

"We have crates of equipment, heavy crates, ten of them." Arthur pointed toward the flatcar. The driver, a man who looked to be in his seventies, eased himself off the wagon seat and shouted an order. Four men came running. They jumped onto the flatcar, pulled up the stakes, and grabbing the rope handles, lifted the crates onto the wagon, and then cinched them down with ropes.

"How do we know these men are the right people, Johannesen?" Flaherty asked.

"We are the right people, señores," answered the driver in English. "We get telegram from Señor Ayles about both you. He says you able to fix the mine."

"We have new parts," Arthur said.

"My name Gutierrez," the driver said. "This my grandson, Tomás. No pay for months. So we need mine fixed."

The visitors continued to look around, entranced by the history.

"Sorry cannot wait, señores. Be dark soon, must make camp in safe place," the driver said as he struggled back into the driver's bench. Arthur and Flaherty jumped aboard and grabbed onto whatever they could. Gutierrez cracked his whip, and they rattled in the direction of the sunset, past a weather-stained cathedral, and scattering children playing with sticks and barrel hoops.

"What is that noise?" asked Arthur.

"Cannon, señor."

"Where are they?" asked Flaherty, his eyes searching under a wrinkling brow.

"Behind us, señor. *Los Federáles*."

"They shoot even when there is nothing to shoot at," said the boy.

The sky darkened, but they kept moving along a road that the driver and the horses knew well. It was a barren land dotted with a few desert scrubs.

Behind the driver and his grandson was a box the width of the wagon. It was secured with an iron lock large enough for a jail. And behind that was a blanket-padded bench on which Arthur and Flaherty rode.

They made camp near a small stream, and Arthur jumped down and washed his face. "I wish we had your Catholic friends and their roast beef now, Flaherty," Arthur said. "I'm hungry."

"Tomás will make a fire," the old man said, "and we will

eat. We are your new Catholic friends. I am hungry, too. The *Federáles*, they suspect everyone, even dogs. Shoot first and ask later. We have to go around them."

Tomás was quick to interrupt. "Los Federáles, they are convicts and criminals, all of them, like Carranza, the President."

The fire of scrub oak twigs and broken branches warmed the evening chill. Out of a leather bag, Tomás pulled a key and unlocked and opened the wagon box. He lifted out a blackened iron kettle and a dented coffee pot, and he filled them both from the canvas water bags.

"Tomas," asked Flaherty, "what is the problem and why is Villa your savior?"

"*La revolución*," said Tomás, "when Villa wins, the people will be free from the corrupt officials and the rich landowners." Flaherty and Arthur listened to Tomás' words, and wrapped their shoulders in blankets from the wagon's box. "He will make the army work three days a week, and on the other three days, train the *pobrecitos* to fight if we are invaded. That is his plan."

The grandfather pulled from his pocket a pad of small papers and made a little trough in one with the fingers of one hand. From another pocket he produced a small sack of tobacco, tapped the leaves into the paper, rolled it into a cigarette, and stuck it in his mouth. "We don't know that, my son. We only hope it will be better," the old man said. "Tomás," the grandfather put a burning twig to the paper tip and pulled on his cigarette, throwing back his head and blowing blue smoke into the night air, "he studied *la historia Norteamericana* in his school. So did I read, in the library. There has been much history since then."

"Grandfather, our hope is with Villa now, you know that. He wants schools for the children." He patted his heart. "And his man, The Hawk, he is strong and will defeat Los Federáles, the enemies of the people."

"Last year," said the grandfather, "Villa was with Carranza, now against. Villa wins some battles, but do we have peace? No."

Arthur and Flaherty listened to the conversation, the voices of youth and of experience disagreeing on urgent and dangerous happenings. The kettle began to boil. Tomás threw in hands full of beans, and squares of meat unwrapped from greasy paper. He tossed in some chili peppers and salt. Into the coffeepot of boiling water, the grandfather sifted two hands full of ground coffee.

"Tomás," the grandfather said, "don't pretend Villa is the Robin Hood. And this hero of yours, The Hawk, last year he fought with Los Federáles, now Villa."

"What is this *revolución* about?" Tomás said. "It is about freedom and just rights. *Como la revolución Norteamericana.*"

"Tomás." The grandfather patted the boy on the shoulder as he looked at his passengers. "His middle name is Jefferson. Tomás Jefferson Gutiérrez. My idea to name him that. Great man Señor Jefferson."

The old man opened a leather case, removed four tin

bowls and wiped them with a rag. They sat cross-legged on the ground, and with a wooden ladle Tomás served the hot beans and meat. They ate with tin spoons and cleaned their bowls with bits of bread and wiped their mouths on their sleeves.

"We just hope," said Arthur, "that we see neither Villa nor the Federáles before we get our job done and get home."

"We are not Americans," Flaherty said. "I'm from Ireland, and he's from Norway."

"Ireland—you have much trouble there, too," said the old man. "I read the papers."

"Aye," Flaherty added, "the Irish know about repression and starvation."

The boy looked at Arthur. "Norway?"

"Norwegians are happy with what they have—work, family, and food. Besides, it's too cold in Norway to worry." He chuckled. "We just get our job done and go to bed." Arthur spooned hot beans into his mouth, wincing.

"If we had jobs, it might be different," added the boy.

From the wagon box, Tomás pulled cotton bedrolls that smelled of campfire smoke and the sweat of men. They kicked off their boots, wrapped themselves into the bed-rolls, and stretched on the grass, side by side. Arthur rolled a blanket for a pillow.

"We have clear nights like this in Ireland, we do," Flaherty said. "I feel for these people."

"I understand. But Flaherty, remember we are here to do a job and get home in two weeks. If we get involved with their war, we may never get home. I have a promise to keep."

"I know how they feel, Johannesen." He smiled and looked over to Arthur wrapped in the bedroll like a cocoon. "Is your father a mechanic like you?"

"No, he is a sea-captain. Big ship with sails and engines. Only saw him once a year. Then he lined us up like sailors and we had to obey orders and keep our toys straight. Always glad to see him go. It was my Uncle Sven who taught me mechanics."

"Like you said, no problems. You're a lucky man."

"Ja vell, maybe." Arthur turned on his side and pulled up the bedroll about his neck.

"It was only last April—the bloody massacre in Dublin. Easter Monday it was."

Arthur watched the dying fire, the sparks drifting into the moonless night and joining the blazing stars. He began to understand his partner's story.

"They don't understand us, the English don't. We are not like them, even if we almost speak the same tongue. They have their social classes. We are just Irishmen. We just want our freedom."

"Uhh, Flaherty." Arthur muttered, listening, but ready for a good sleep.

"Sean, my brother, only fourteen, he was just curious, just standing there with a flag. The English soldiers shot him. His friends tried to pull him away, and they shot them, too." Flaherty paused, took a deep breath, sighed. "He bled to death right there on the street. Only fourteen." Flaherty choked back a word and cleared his throat. "Do you see why I came to America, Johannesen? No repression. Freedom. Peace. A chance to make my own way. Why I care?" He turned to Arthur, "I hope you understand?"

Arthur was wide-eyed now and unable to respond for a moment, then said, "Ja, I do." Arthur paused more and stared into the night. "Flaherty, I am so sorry to hear this. I do understand." Arthur left it at that, not able to add a thing. But he was getting to know this Irishman.

Chapter Nine
The Card Players

"We will get to La Promesa before sundown, señores," said Tomás, sitting next to his grandfather on the driver's bench as they continued their trek. The
morning cool evaporated into a dry heat that burned their
faces. At this latitude and altitude the sun was an intense
companion.

Tomas held the reins to the straining horses in his left hand
while Grandfather Gutierrez snoozed under his sombrero, his
body rocking in lazy patterns as the wagon climbed higher
in the Sierra Madre foothills west of Parral. An eagle circled
overhead, riding the warm rising currents. The wagon creaked,
the iron-rimmed wheels crunched against the stones, and the
horses strained and snorted, but the men were silent.

Stopping by a cold stream, they filled the water bags,
opened the wagon's box and ate cold tortillas and cheese.
Arthur patted the crates and counted them again as if one
may have vanished. He nodded his head and said, "Soon I

hope. It is taking us three days to get to the mine, not two. Ayles was wrong."

"Maybe Ayles has never been here," said Flaherty. "We didn't ask him that."

"We didn't know what to ask," said Arthur.

The sun was lowering. The road snaked into a valley, and at the head of it, where the road turned to go down the other side, was an adobe church that could hold no more than about thirty people. The late afternoon sun washed one side of the crumbling stucco. The tower, its bell gone, cast a long shadow on the graveyard with its crooked head-stones and weathered dates and names from times past. The graveyard was filled with weeds, except for one fresh mound of shoveled dirt topped by a bouquet of wilted flowers and presided over by a straight headstone with fresh carving. Flaherty squinted and leaned forward to read the marker, but from the jiggling wagon, the name was illegible as they rounded the curve and moved away.

Gutierrez wiped his forehead and pointed at the grave, "Señor Abercrombie. You heard, no?"

"Abercrombie?" Arthur snapped a look at Flaherty. "That was the name Ayles said, right? The last manager of the mine?"

"Is that right, Gutierrez?" Flaherty repeated. "The manager?"

"*Sí*. Eight months he work here."

"When——how long ago?"

"Only two weeks now he die. Two weeks before he

in bed and no work." The wagon rattled down the road. Flaherty looked back at the church.

"How did it happen? Shot?"

"Ha, no señores," said the old man, "whiskey and woman. Too much whiskey and wrong woman."

"But, yes, grandfather, he was shot," Tomás said.

"It was whiskey that got him shot, Tomás. The police chief's daughter. *El gringo loco!*" The Grandfather poked his head with a finger.

Around the next curve they saw it. Three buildings at angles to each other enclosed within a broken rock and adobe wall the height of a man. The gates, double gates of iron, were hanging crooked and open in the weeds, looking as if they had never been closed.

"*La Promesa*, señores," the driver pointed—but then shouted, "But, wait!" Gutierrez pulled up the horses, stopped, and pointed towards the mine. "Colonel Herrera again."

Arthur shaded his eyes with his hand, squinting into the sun. "Who's Herrera?" Disappearing in a cloud of dust were the rear ends of horses and the backs of men in white uniforms.

Tomás gripped his rifle. "Federáles Colonel, he makes the big trouble."

The grandfather added, "Herrera shot the Mexican crew because they could not get the mine fixed after Ayles left last time."

"Ayles, last time?" said Arthur.

"They were good men, my friends," said Tomás.

Above on the hillside was a long adobe and frame structure with a small tower with tangled ropes hanging about. It sat a stone's throw from the mouth of a ragged man-sized hole in the side of one of two peaks that shadowed the camp.

"It looks abandoned, Gutierrez," said Flaherty.

"No señor, some people here. You meet."

Chickens squawked and flapped out of their way.

Through the sagging gates, they pulled up beside a green planked door in one of the buildings. It was a square building about a hundred feet on each side with adobe walls two feet thick. On the flagpole outside hung a pulley, but no flag and no rope. Through one of the windows, a yellow light shone.

"Tomás," said the grandfather, "take our friends inside. I will find help and unload the crates at the mine house."

Tomás held open the heavy door and Arthur and Flaherty stepped into a room where four men sat playing cards at one end of a table under a smoking kerosene lamp with circling moths. No one seemed to notice the strangers. The air smelled of liquor, burning kerosene, and tobacco smoke.

"Señores," Tomás called, "visitors."

One man turned to see the newcomers, a Chinese man in a dirty white smock. Out the back of his skull cap a black pigtail hung to his waist. He waved his hand of cards in the air and said, "How do, gent'men. We know you come, ha."

Arthur and Flaherty approached the table; the yellow

lamplight illumined their faces. The Chinese man stood up and nodded a quick bow. "How do, gent'men. I cook. Name Carlos, *por favor*. Ha." He laid his cards face down and pointed to the others. "Dis man, Heinz, he engineer." He shook his finger at another. "Dis man, he name Smytha. He geo-gist."

"Greetings," said Smythe, squinting into the dark at the newcomers. "You're more welcome than the visitors who just left." He had streaked long blond hair and a smile that seemed to turn up only at the edges of his mouth.

"Welcome," said Heinz. He nodded his head—brown hair streaked with grey.

"Welcome to Mexico, señores," said the last man. He was short, muscular, and had a black patch over his left eye. "I am Commandante Sanchez, Chief of Police in this district. We have gotten used to Colonel Herrera. Don't worry."

"My name is Flaherty, Michael Flaherty. Mr. Johannesen here," and he turned to Arthur, "is the expert in mining operations."

The men at the table exchanged noncommittal looks. Smythe returned to his cards.

"Arthur Johannesen," the Norwegian said, "I come from Phelps Dodge in Arizona. We will be here only long enough to fix the mine, few weeks."

The Police Chief smiled and glanced at the other faces. "That is what Abercrombie said when he came," said Sanchez. "Mr. Joh…, sorry, Señor, what is your name again?"

"Jo-han-nes-sen."

The others dropped their eyes and studied their cards.

"Well, gentlemen, we are going to do our best, we are," Flaherty said. "We promised Mr. Ayles that."

"Oh yes, Ayles," said Smythe and he shook his head. "Your call, Heinz."

"I show you room, gent'men," said the Chinese cook.

"What about the bloody game, Carlos?" Smythe called.

"Have drink. I back soon."

"Señores," said Sanchez, "Mr. Ayles told you mine broken down, *si*?"

"We brought new parts, Señor Sanchez," Flaherty said.

"*Imposible. Mina muy* broken." The Police Chief waved his hand in finality. Heinz and Smythe focused, like they were deaf, on the cards .

Arthur felt the silence strange and unnerving. He glanced at them for a moment, but Carlos interrupted the awkward-delay and pointed toward the door.

Carlos led them to a dark wooden building, opened the door and said, "Sorry, gent'men, one room for both you. Water bucket here." He pointed to the washstand and bowl. "Pump outside." He pointed out the door. "Crapper out-side. Bring own paper."

"It is not quite the Paso Del Norte, Arthur," said Flaherty, "but better than the one in Jiménez."

Arthur smiled. "Thank you, Carlos."

"Dinner soon, gent'men. Come back Casa Grande tirty *minutos*. Ha."

The beds were two wooden cots with woven leather straps, each with a thin mattress with cotton peeking out the open seams. Three blankets and a pillow were folded on the foot of each cot. A wooden table scarred like a butcher's block stood in the corner with three chairs, one with no back. Moths flitted about a kerosene lantern hanging from a hook in the center of the room.

"You take that one, Flaherty." Arthur pointed to the bed under the picture of the crucifixion. Otherwise the walls were bare. A small lizard in the open window blinked its eyes and scooted over the sill.

Back at the Casa Grande, they were still playing cards, even Carlos. A boy stirred a pot in the open kitchen. "Take Carlo's hand, Flaherty," said Smythe. "He has to get supper. It's just poker, and we play for pesos."

Flaherty took the cook's chair and picked up his cards, brushing away a moth.

Arthur wandered out the open door into the night. The stars sparkled, and he wondered at the number and depth of space. But the sky was different that the northern heavens of Norway. He remembered his science teacher, strict and frowning Mr. Arnesen, and the stories of how Galileo fought against the Church to defend his teachings of the sun-centered solar system and the moons of Jupiter. Arthur thought of his family home outside Kristiania, the hammock in the garden. His mother and sister, and how strict they both were on him, as Lutheran mothers and sisters will be. There were no men at home now. Had he done the wrong thing in leaving? He drew a deep breath of the cool evening air and pulled the gold locket from his shirt pocket, caressing it between his fingers. He popped it open, brought it to his lips, and thought of his dear Pauline and the promised comforts of El Paso. Then he reached in his pocket again, pulling out the letter. It was wrinkled and now stained with sweat. It was too dark to read, but he knew every word of it; that she felt his love, his commitment, and that she felt safe with him. He wasn't going to lose this one. El Paso seemed so far away. Maybe she had a good idea—a job with her father couldn't be that bad. "I'll be home soon," he whispered to her picture and clicked the locket shut. He kissed the locket and letter and returned them to the warmth of his pocket.

"Supper, Johannesen," Flaherty called out the door.

Another lamp had been lit over the scarred wood supper table where six places were set. Heinz, the German, spoke first. "You are not Americans?"

The kitchen boy brought a pot of steaming soup and ladled it into the tin bowls.

"Irish," said Flaherty and he touched his heart.

"I'm from Norway," said Arthur, "in America two years."

"We heard from Ayles," said Heinz, "that you are a mining engineer."

"Not a mining engineer, Mr. Heinz, a mechanic."

Sanchez slurped his soup. It was sausage, vegetables and chilies.

"Like I told you," Heinz said in his German accent, "it seems a mine destined not to be fixed."

"Then why has Mr. Ayles sent us here?" asked Flaherty.

Smythe lifted his head from the soup and with a sneer of the upper lip said to Flaherty, "You should bloody well ask Mr. Ayles."

The kitchen boy put a plate of fried chicken and a bowl of *pintos* on the table, and the men dug in with their forks and spoons. Carlos served a pitcher of beer and another of coffee.

"Can anyone here," asked Arthur, "give us a hand in the morning. Information about the mine machinery would help, too."

"Heinz here," said Sanchez, "he is engineer."

The kitchen boy laid a platter of tortillas on the table and a bowl of oranges. They continued the supper in silence. Finally Heinz said, "Tomorrow, Mr. Johannesen. Have a good rest."

Chapter Ten
Whose Gold?

*A*rthur rose with the sun and climbed the hill to the machine shed before anyone else was even awake. He paused and surveyed the area. From the gaping mine entrance ran a pair of iron rails to a point where a conveyor belt had been, only broken rollers now in the dirt. No ore cart was in sight. Arthur pushed open the big wooden shutters on the side of the shed for the sun and air. The wooden cases from Zork filled the room. Finding a rusty crowbar in the corner under greasy rags, he pried open all the cases, removed the nails, and arranged the top boards flat on the dirt outside, so there would be a clean place to inspect the parts. Laying out first the tools he had ordered at Zork; the screwdrivers, wrenches, torches, hammers, emery cloth, all in a neat order, he stood back with a clean rag in one hand and a pipe wrench in the other, and surveyed the job ahead. He wiped the perspiration from his brow with the rag. He recorded his first steps of this job, the date and time, in his notebook. The sun was well up when Flaherty walked up rubbing his eyes.

"Carlos said breakfast is getting cold," said Flaherty. "He says it's at nine since no one has to work, because the mine is down."

Arthur laid down the wrench, wiped his hands on the rag, and followed Flaherty down the hill to the Casa Grande.

At the table was the breakfast of tortillas, scrambled eggs with chili, and big white mugs of coffee, and places set for the two new men. Arthur removed his hat, ran his hand though his hair and sat down.

"Good sleep, gentlemen?" asked Smythe. When Smythe spoke it was with a constant smile, more of a smirk out the corner of his mouth, as if he knew something others did not.

"Good enough, Mr. Smythe," said Arthur and he rolled a tortilla and took a bite. "I have already unpacked the parts."

"I will be up to help you soon," Heinz said. "Did you hear the cannons last night?"

Flaherty stopped his fork of eggs half-way to his mouth. "Cannons?"

Arthur stopped chewing.

"Not to worry, gent'men," Carlos added. "Far away, near Rosarita town. Sound go far at night."

Arthur finished his mouthful of eggs and washed it down with a gulp of coffee. "We have new parts and it should take no more than two, three days to get it running again."

"Do you know what's wrong?" asked Smythe.

"Looks like we have to start from—what you call it? From scratch? Not a problem."

"Do you hear cannon every night?" Flaherty looked around the room for an answer.

"Only when they come this way," said Smythe. "We haven't seen either side since, what, yesterday?" Smythe looked at Flaherty and smiled.

Heinz nodded. "It's the Federáles who have the cannon."

Arthur wiped his mouth with the napkin, picked up his hat, and said, "Excuse me, gentlemen," and left the table, his plate still half full, and climbed back up to the mine.

With hands on hips, the Norwegian surveyed the mess of damaged machinery lying about the shed.

"*Buenos dias*, señor," a young voice said. Tomás Jefferson Gutierrez stood in his clean white pants and rope belted tunic, the uniform of the Mexican *campesino*, a country peasant.

"Ah, good day, Tomás." Arthur removed his hat and scratched his head.

"You need help, señor?"

"I am supposed to have a helper, but he is still drinking his coffee. Ja vell, I have to find out what is broken, Tomás, and then see if any of this can fix it." He continued to inspect the machinery. "Let's start with this shaft. The old one is missing. Why do you think that was?"

"To stop the machinery from working, señor." Tomás picked up the oil can. "You will find it in the canyon."

"And this reduction gear…" Arthur kicked it with his boot. "…I have never seen one broken like this."

"They used the hammer there, señor," and Tomás pointed to a sledge hammer standing in the corner.

"Who is 'they,' Tomas?"

Flaherty arrived up the hill from the Casa Grande, sweating in the growing heat. He picked up the other end of the shaft. "Did you hear about the party, Johannesen?"

"It should fit just here," said Arthur. They moved the shaft end to the coupling. Arthur, puzzled, looked at Flaherty as if the Irishman had the answer. "It is too short," Arthur said in disgust.

Tomás said, "Everyone wants the gold, señor. Villa and the Federáles and the American owner. And everyone wants to stop the others from getting it. So they break it."

"The party is Friday night," Flaherty said, "Chief Sanchez's daughter. Getting married. Everyone will be there. We're invited."

"Let's try the other end," Arthur said and the boy helped. The other end didn't fit either, and Arthur sat down and opened his shirt and rolled up his sleeves.

"See these two gears, Flaherty? There is supposed to be a third one." Arthur went outside and picked up the reduction gear with both hands and wrestled it into the shack.

"I hear he has two daughters," said Flaherty.

"Si, Señor," said Tomás, holding the oil can now, "the

youngest one is champion horse woman. Beats all the men—even her older brother. She is the one getting married."

"Look at this, Flaherty." Arthur had slipped the reduction gear onto its spindle, but its teeth didn't touch the other two gears. "These are the most important parts, Flaherty. They don't fit, eh?" Arthur turned over a bucket and sat on it, wiping the sweat off his face. He pulled out his notebook, scribbled a few sentences and put it back in his pocket. "My uncle Sven would laugh at this and walk away. How can a country become a proper nation if it mistreats its machines, eh?"

Flaherty said, "It's how it treats its sons and daughters that count."

"Will you listen to me, Flaherty? I don't care if the Chief has twenty daughters. We have a problem, you and I, the two of us—a machine problem. Already almost a week has passed and you are talking about a party."

Flaherty listened and nodded.

"Parties don't get us home and paid," Arthur continued. "That is all we are here for. Agree?" Arthur's face reddened. He licked his lips. A glance at Flaherty's blue and green plaid pants, brought a response.

"I'll change, I have another pair for work."

A new face struggled up the hill. It was Smythe. "Got it fixed yet, Norwegian?"

"These damn parts don't fit," said Arthur, turning from his Irish helper. "This is a mess."

"Doesn't surprise me a bit," Smythe smiled. "That's

Ayles for you."

Flaherty straightened, "What do you suggest we do, Mr. Smythe."

"That should be clear to both of you."

"We don't break an agreement, Mr. Smythe. Do you have a helpful suggestion for us?"

"Go back where you come from, Mr. Flaherty," he said with a curl of his lip.

Flaherty hesitated, turned away, then turned back and said, "Be ready for a surprise, Mr. Smythe. Come, Tomás." The two walked away. "We are going back where we came from and wait for lunch."

"Mr. Smythe," asked Arthur, "why did you say that to my partner? We were just ready to get moving."

"Why are you two here, anyway? A Norwegian and," Smythe looked down the hill, "a bloody Irishman." Smythe ran his hand through his long hair and shifted his feet, standing with his narrow black braces supporting his soiled gray trousers.

"We made a contract, together," said Arthur, "and we will do our job."

"Contract, ha! There is a war going on." Smythe looked out of the top of his eyes. "Are you aware of that?"

"You mean in Mexico or in France? Norway is neutral in both," Arthur said.

"Well, it shouldn't be," said Smythe with his cynical smile. "All of us should fight the bloody Huns, America included."

"Well, Mr. Smythe, I am happy I have no say in that."

Smythe turned to go downhill. "Best you don't, Mr. Johannesen. Just keep fiddling with your machinery. You will tire and give up—just like the others. Or end up like Abercrombie." He tipped his head up the canyon toward the church and grave.

"What others did is of no concern to me, Smythe. Although the parts don't fit, it is also clear to me what is wrong, and I tell you—it is not impossible. I know what has to be done."

Arthur watched the Englishman leave, shook his head in disgust, spat on the ground, then turned to his parts and the machine, his hat in his hand and his hands on his hips, "Yes, my friend, be ready for a surprise. Things aren't always as they seem."

After supper, Flaherty passed on the card game. They both turned in early.

"That fellow Smythe," Arthur said, "He is an unhappy man, eh?"

"That's his problem," said Flaherty. "I came to America to get away from his sort. I try to hold no grudges, but how can we win the war with narrow minds like his on our side. He should be sent to France, to the trenches. Then he would learn responsibility to others."

"And what," said Arthur, "is he doing here? Who is paying him? And Heinz? Who is paying him? The only place where Germans and English are facing each other is in France."

"And here in Mexico it seems," said Flaherty.

"Ja vell, we'll find out why in time," said Arthur and he poked his finger at the Irishman's chest. "Tomorrow I will need your help. Some heavy lifting. I think I have it figured out. But we may need a little creativity."

"That may be the easiest thing to do," the Irishman said.

Chapter Eleven
What About Heinz?

"The name is Heinz, Wolfgang Heinz."

Arthur turned, greeted the German and shook his hand. It was a firm hand, Arthur noted. "Ja, I remember," he said.

The sun was long up and it was past eight. Arthur had been studying the problem, the broken machinery and the misfit parts, for over an hour.

"You are a mining engineer, Mr. Heinz?"

"You might say so, Mr. Johannesen. University of Heidelberg. My home, too." Heinz was a hefty man, taller than Arthur, in his forties, with a short gray streaked beard that matched his hair and dark bushy eyebrows over gray eyes that Arthur thought conveyed a hint of kindness.

"So far away. Mexico," said Arthur.

"My family used to summer in Norway," said Heinz. "On the West Coast. Ålesund. Do you know it?"

"Ja, beautiful fjords and mountains," said Arthur. "Why are you here?"

"I have a job to do," Heinz said. "Like you. How can I help you?"

"So what is your job, Mr. Heinz?"

"I have interests to keep my eye on. It's complicated."

"There is a big war In Europe. Does it have to do with that war? The one over there?"

"Hard to explain, Mr. Johannesen. We're all involved in these wars whether we like it or not. "

"Well, I don't want to get involved in other's problems. The world is too big for all that."

"If I were you, I'd feel the same way."

"But, what does your country, Germany have to do with this mess in Mexico? Is this your interest, Mr. Heinz?"

Heinz took a breath, looked about at the machinery and parts, and didn't answer.

Arthur began to tear two-inch strips of the emery cloth. "Just to get back to El Paso soon as I make this machine work, that's all I want. My interest is up north." He stood back and started pointing. "You know how this works, Mr. Heinz. That diesel engine runs the gears that take ore from the mine on a long belt that dumps it into this crusher with the gears that don't fit on that shaft that is too short." He shrugged his shoulders. "Is that how it is supposed to work, Mr. Heinz? You have seen it working, eh?"

"Yes, you have a big challenge, Mr. Johannesen," Heinz said, nodding his head in agreement.

Arthur picked up a handful of the crushed ore in a corner.

"I think this is good gold ore, don't you agree?"

"I am told its high quality," the German said.

"You will see, Mr. Heinz, this machinery will soon again crush this fine ore."

"Ah," called Flaherty, puffing from the climb. "Good morning to you, Mr. Heinz." He sat down on an overturned can. "Will you be going to the Chief's party for his daughter tomorrow?"

"I will, Mr. Flaherty," said Heinz. "These parties last for days, and afterwards you won't worry about the mine for a while." The German laughed and said, "If you have any real heavy lifting, call on me." That was the first time they had seen him smile.

By afternoon, Arthur had found that some of the smaller parts actually did fit and some were not needed. With a long pry bar he and Flaherty inched one section closer to the other so the short shaft would reach. He had tried several different gears so that now, although the ratios were different, they touched each other and would turn. But, they could do nothing about the distance from the shed to the hole in the mountain. There was no belt and it had to be thirty feet long to reach the end of the protruding rails.

"How could a responsible manager," he asked Flaherty, "let his equipment get in such a bad condition, and then order such parts, all wrong?"

"Maybe he didn't," replied Flaherty. "Wasn't that him in the graveyard we passed?"

Chapter Twelve
The Far Reach of the Somme

Arthur and Flaherty, in their sweaty undershirts, stepped out of the machinery shed. It was the middle of the afternoon. Arthur wiped his face with his red bandana.

"I need a beer, Flaherty," he said.

A shadow drifted over the site and thunderheads began to rise in mountainous heights to the west, hiding the sun. A breeze brought the scent of pine and juniper down the slope. The weather change brought a hope of mechanical change and up the hill came young Tomás with a jug.

"You should take care, señor," said Tomás. "Every afternoon clouds get bigger and blacker and then one day—boom! The devil beats his wife, we say."

"Well, Tomás, we could use that rain," Flaherty said. "It's hotter than Hades."

"Then it doesn't rain again for five or six days," Tomás said. "I brought you some cool water. We keep it cool in box under the floor."

Arthur patted the boy on his back. "*Gracias*, Tomás."

"That's thunder, isn't it," asked Flaherty. "Not cannons?" The hollow booming sounds were distant and the air cooling.

Arthur wiped the tools with a clean rag. "If you want to go to that party tomorrow, Flaherty, we have to finish what we started today." He remembered for a moment those same words his Uncle Sven used on him the discipline of finishing the job before he could join his friends for fun.

They returned to the machinery shed, and the sounds of hammering, grunting, and swearing in two languages replaced the thunder. Golden shafts of the evening sun reached from the canyons of the receding storm clouds.

At the supper table later the same men sat in the same chairs, with the same food as the night before. Arthur filled his tortilla with beans and shredded meat, and watched the others. Even Flaherty was quiet, busy with the food.

"Sorry, Smy-tha, bad news," said Carlos.

"Yes, Carlos, very bad indeed," Smythe said with an aggressive tone and he glared at Heinz. "Sixty thousand Englishmen in one day. Bloody criminal."

Heinz was quiet, looking at his plate, his fork pushing the beans about.

Arthur and Flaherty looked up in question and stopped chewing. "What's this all about?" asked Arthur.

Heinz looked at the Englishman. "The war was not my idea, Mr. Smythe."

"The newspaper from Parral, señores," explained Carlos,

and he shook the wrinkled days-old paper in the air.

Tomás quietly translated for Arthur and Flaherty. "It is about a big battle, señores, called Battle of the Somme, the English soldiers, sixty thousand die first day."

The foreigners looked at each other. *"Sixty thousand!"* whispered Arthur. They looked at Smythe and shook their heads in disbelief. "How can that happen?"

Tomás continued, "Paper say battle lines between German and English and French armies go six hundred miles across France, and the Allies losing."

"The Allies are not all there yet," said Smythe. "One Ally must come in to tip the scales, to free Europe from this unwanted scourge."

"You mean America, sí?" said Carlos.

"Sí," said Smythe.

Heinz had no comment and pushed his remaining beans around with his fork. This did not appear to be news to Heinz, and Arthur wondered what he knew and how he knew it."

Carlos the cook placed a big bowl of stewed apples on the table. "So gent-men. The big fiesta *mañana*, ha!"

Chapter Thirteen
Unexpected Guests

"You put your foot in the stirrup like this," Flaherty said.

"I rode a horse in Arizona," replied Arthur. "I know how to do it." He grabbed the stirrup, stuck his booted foot in it, reached up with one hand and grabbed the saddle horn. The horse, a flea-bitten gray covered with scabs, sidled away from the Norwegian. Arthur held onto the horn and hopped on one foot alongside the animal, until the beast reversed direction and rammed its barrel belly into the Norwegian. Arthur seized the saddle with his free hand, threw his leg over the top, and struggled into the seat.

The men in the wagon hooted and laughed. "You are facing the right way, señor," called Tomás. "Now whisper in the horse's ear where to go."

Everyone was going to the party; Carlos the Chinese cook and his helper, even Smythe, all in the wagon. The only one missing was Heinz.

The *Dos Gringos,* as they were now called by the Mexicans, looked out of place on their horses, blond Arthur an awkward soldier in his khakis and cavalryman's hat, and Flaherty a clown with his red hair, although he didn't wear his plaid pants on this trip. Flaherty and Arthur trotted behind the wagon along the trail through the pass, brushing scrub pines and live oak on one side and avoiding the cavernous drop on the other. They passed abandoned mines, their buildings a pile of broken adobe, weathered boards, and bent bolts where the equipment had been. After four hours and over the hills onto a wider road, they stopped for a rest at an old café. *La Cantina Rosa,* the sign read. A handwritten note pinned on the door said the owner was in town for the wedding and fiesta.

"The fiesta there." Tomás pointed to the village in the distant valley. "Famous town, Santa Barbara. Where Spanish Viceroy ruled all land to the north," and he waved his arm like a tour director, "from Texas to California. Gold was discovered way back—in 1500s," he said. "But now just quiet village, like an old worn-out man, one time a king but cannot remember when. Now only pretty green hills." That day in late August the village silence was broken by the sounds of happiness, of the Commandante's daughter getting married.

Red, white, and green banners fluttered from the elm trees and in the plaza in front of the church. Everywhere was the happy sound of the Mariachis with their guitars, trumpets, and men singing. The visitors from La Promesa mine were late. The bride in her white gown and crown of flowers and the groom in his black suit and confused expression were already being feted. "We haven't missed the party, thank goodness," said Flaherty.

The Norwegian and the Irishman gathered welcoming looks from the partygoers and foreigners returned the smiles. The locals were in their finest, the women in long yellow or red skirts and low-cut white blouses. The gentlemen in black suits like businessmen, some in the silver-bangled pants and jackets of the *mariachi*, and the peasants, the *campesinos*, in their sandals and white *camisas* under red, green, and blue *serapes*—every man with a glass or bottle in his hand.

Tomás jumped down from the wagon, "Hurry, señores, good food." They tied up the horses on a dirt side street stacked with bales of hay. The tables were loaded with fruit, bowls of beans, and platters of tortillas. The older women brought platters of tamales, *machaca* dried beef, and *Barbacoa de Lomo*, barbequed steak wrapped in maguey leaves. On every table were bottles of tequila, beer, and a local mezcal wine.

"Look at Commandante Sanchez," said smiling Tomás. "Father of the bride, so proud." The Chief of Police strutted like a tom-turkey in his crisp khaki uniform, black belt, brass buckles, black eye patch, and red and blue badges of authority. It was the wedding of Nina his youngest daughter to Roberto the son of a local rancher.

Flaherty whispered in Tomás's ear, "Is that the daughter Abercrombie was chasing?"

"No, señor, she is there," he said and pointed to a tall, dark-eyed woman who stood straight and confident like a ballerina. "That is Juanita, the older one. No husband, yet." Heinz and Smythe and the others drifted into the crowd. Arthur stood expressionless, exchanging looks with Juanita Sanchez. She smiled. He smiled. He found it hard not to. She was a piece of art.

Arthur and Flaherty had their fill of *chilorio, chalupos, mole poblano* and enjoyed the *menudo norteña,* until they discovered it was a soup of tripe.

"The girls are pretty, don't you think, Johannesen? If I could only speak their damn language."

Arthur, with more tequila than he expected to drink, sat on the ground with his back against the rough trunk of an ancient elm, smiling, surprised at his enjoyment of the music, the dancing, the happy people, the food, so strange with its variety of spices, and the pretty girls. He was ready to catch sight of Juanita again, but she had disappeared, at least from the view where he sat at the tree base.

"Enjoy yourself," Flaherty said. "You are single now. Married later."

Arthur stood, dusting himself off. He heard, *"Buenas tardes, señor."* It was a woman's voice, soft with a lilt at the end of her greeting. He looked around and saw Juanita, searching for an answer and then he squeezed out, *"Buenas tardes, señorita."*

"El dia está agredáble, sí?" Juanita said and waved her arms at the sky, *"para la fiesta para mi hermana."*

"Sí," said Arthur, nodding and looking at the sky.

"*Satisfecho?*" She rubbed her belly.

"Sí," Arthur said wondering what he had just agreed to.

Juanita looked around, as if afraid of being caught talking to a stranger without a proper introduction. But she continued speaking in Spanish to him. Arthur wished he understood as she sounded like an intelligent woman. But all he could say was "sí" and a few "buenos" and that was getting him nowhere. His mind flashed back to Pauline's warning about the pretty senoritas. Then Juanita's head jerked to the left, and she did a double take at the new arrivals at the edge of the square. She stiffened and stepped back.

Arthur saw there were only two. From his position they looked like giants. They sat high on their horses, one a black horse and the other a sorrel. "Hey, Flaherty," he called to the Irishman who was talking to a young woman up close as if telling her a secret. "Look at those men," Arthur nodded toward the far end of the Plaza.

Then there were four well-armed men on horseback and soon Arthur lost count as saw over twelve of them he thought. Big sombreros, belts of cartridges crossing their chests, and each mustachioed man had two pistols hanging from his waist and several rifles or carbines secured to his saddle in carved leather scabbards. These men sat silently on their horses, like princes, watching. The wedding party began to notice the new visitors and quieted down almost to a silence.

In front of the unsmiling troop, a man trotted out on a palomino the color of a fourteen-carat coin. The rider carried only one Winchester carbine strapped to his silver inlaid saddle, but two pearl handled Colts hung from his hips. He tipped his hat, not a sombrero, but a wide-brimmed Stetson, and said, *"Buenas tardes, mis amigos. El Halcón deseales una feliz fiesta."* He gestured with his hat toward the bride and groom, *"Y una vida muy agredáble, en un nuevo Mexico."*

With such greetings and good wishes, Arthur sensed a relaxing sigh from the crowd. The man on the palomino dismounted and strode to the main table. Commandante Sanchez poured a small glass of mescal for the honored guest, The Hawk, who held it high toward the newlyweds, and said, *"Buena salud, buena fortuna, y felicidad y el mejor deseo de El Halcón y el Generál Villa."*

Men raised their glasses and shouted, *"Viva Roberto y Nina, Viva El Halcón, Viva Villa."* The Commandante motioned toward the food. With a quick signal, The Hawk's men dismounted, and now smiling under their sweeping mustaches, joined the party. The mariachis were louder, the dancing happier, and no one lacked for food or drink.

Chapter Fourteen
The Storm

At first the cooling breeze was unnoticed by the crowd. When Arthur looked to its source, he saw black thunderheads in the west boiling upwards like smoke from a volcano. The thunder rumblings increased and began to drown the guitars and trumpets, but few noticed. The sky turned dark as if the sun had burned out. Arthur looked for Flaherty and Tomás, but before he took ten steps, the whole town lit up like the inside of an exploding star. Fingers of fire danced about the church steeple, and the acrid smell of ozone filled the air. People ran like frightened chickens once they see the fox.

The rain came in one big swoosh like somewhere in heaven a dam had broken. Flaherty, Tomás, and his grandfather crowded inside the church with the others. The bride's hair dripped about her shoulders, her flower crown wilted. Arthur squeezed inside the church door for the rain to pass. It didn't.

The deluge settled down to a steady pour as if those clouds had been holding it in for weeks, which was nearly right as the storm came in the late afternoon just as Tomás had predicted a few days earlier. "Ay, it is the devil beating his wife, no?" Tomás said again.

Arthur felt uncomfortable, surrounded by paintings of a suffering Jesus with a crown of thorns, of tearful women, and the darkness. It was all very new to him, a Lutheran. Boys were running around lighting candles.

The Hawk and some of his men were in the church, slapping their hats against their legs to shake off the water. Some were strolling, looking important, and others melted into the crowd. Tomás whispered to Arthur and Flaherty. "That's him, The Hawk. I told you about him before. He is our hero."

"We know," said Arthur, remembering what the nuns had warned and the murders the El Paso newspaper had reported. Grandfather Gutierrez was seated in a pew rubbing his leg.

The Hawk, repositioning his wet Stetson on his head, turned and looked at Arthur out the corner of his eye. He straightened his belt with the Colts and walked toward the Norwegian. "Señor," he said and shook his head up and down in an approving way. "I have heard much of you." He nodded up and down more. "You are the master mechanic who will fix our mine, no?" The Hawk looked around and waited for an answer. "Welcome to our country, señor mechanic. We can use a man of your skills."

Gathering now were more of The Hawks men, nodding in agreement with their chief. Arthur looked about seeing he was surrounded and felt a chill. Tomás and Flaherty backed against the wall. Tomás smiled and jiggled his head to get Arthur to agree to anything the Villista said. Arthur took a breath, put on a slight but steady smile and said, "La Promesa mine is in good hands, Señor Hawk."

The Hawk focused on Tomás and the Irishman. Slowly pulling one of his pearl-handled Colts from its holster and while everyone held their breaths, The Hawk twirled it about his middle finger, laughed, lifted it to his hair and without disturbing his hat, scratched his head with the gun's muzzle. "It's good to hear that, señor," he said. "We will be around to see the work of those hands." He looked around and smiled. "For sure, next time we will not meet in a church. The storm is over. Let's enjoy."

He spun the Colt again and dropped it in the holster. He headed for the door and everyone followed. But Arthur sat down in a pew, took a deep breath, looked about the walls with Jesus on the cross.

Tomás and Flaherty remained against the wall. "Impressive man, your Hawk, Tomás," Flaherty said.

"We are so honored to have him here," said Tomás and leaned closer to the Irishman. "Señor," Tomás said, "I heard what you say to Señor Johannesen the night we slept under the stars on the way to the mine. That was a terrible price to pay."

Flaherty looked at the boy, the age of his lost brother, and who in a few years would be taller than his rifle.

"Yes, my friend, a terrible and unnecessary price to pay." The Irishman looked around and saw Arthur standing in the door, looking out at the diminished crowd.

"Sí, señor, the price of freedom. We know that in México. Your brother was killed by the English soldiers."

"That's not the whole story, Tomás." They sat in a pew and the boy leaned forward to not miss a word. "The soldiers on the street were shooting at me, Tomás. I was waving the glorious flag of Irish freedom." In the air he outlined the shape of a flag with his hands. "The green flag with the golden harp. When the soldiers came around the corner, they shot at me. I was doing all the yelling, feeling important."

"You a brave man, señor."

"No, Tomás. I wasn't. I ran."

Tomás was silent, unbelieving, and he looked around to see if anyone else heard.

"I not only ran, Tomás, I dropped the flag. My brother picked it up and waved it high. The English bullets hit him instead of me. I ran, Tomás. Do you understand?"

"No, I don't."

"Never run, my boy. You will never run far enough after that."

The Mexican boy straightened and looked into Flaherty's face and then, after a moment said, "Is Mexico far enough, señor?"

The thunder was receding, but at times a new flash appeared out of nowhere, and the ground trembled with the following roar. A few people jumped back into the church or ran for other cover. Arthur turned and joined Flaherty and Tomás. The young Mexican nodded toward the departed hero. "El Halcón is a great patriot, the honest and fair man," he said, "but we know never to cross him or we will never have a second chance."

"Ja, if you say so my friend. But I just as soon we not meet again, church or no church."

"The fiesta will continue," Flaherty said, "but wet. All these girls, and all I can do is wink at them."

"Ja," said Arthur and he laughed. "I know what you mean." He looked about but no Juanita. "We should head home. We have lots of work to do."

"Very dark soon, señores," said Tomás.

"I think we can find our way," Flaherty said, "and the moon may come out. It was almost full last night."

"Take care, señores. Grandfather and I will follow you."

Arthur looked about the church. He saw only puddles on the green tiled floor.

The horses were stomping their hooves and jerking

at their tethers, still nervous from the storm, but Flaherty talked to them like friends and petted their necks. Pulling ponchos from the saddle bags to protect from the occasional sprinkles, Arthur said "Ja, let's go," and mounted the wet saddle with a new found confidence. In the western sky now were hints of golden light as they began to retrace their earlier trip.

Chapter Fifteen
Targets

The golden sun slipped below the clouds and mountains, but without its usual fiery ceremony. The sky darkened, the air fresh and still full of the smell of rain. In their ponchos and hats, Arthur and Flaherty began to cross a log bridge over a ravine filled with the raging waters from the sudden rain and approached La Cantina Rosa again. Dark on their way into Santa Barbara, now a yellow light beamed from a window and through the open door. They could see men talking. Four figures were silhouetted in that light. Arthur held out his hand and motioned Flaherty to stop. "Shhh, listen," Arthur whispered. Even over the sound of the rushing creek, the voices were audible. "Listen. You hear that, Flaherty? German! They're talking German."

"It's Heinz!" said Flaherty a bit too loudly.

"And that man again. At Zork. In the black suit and homburg," said Arthur.

A weak flash of sheet lightning danced across the

sky, long enough for Arthur and Flaherty to confirm the identity of the men at the door, their heads together in conversation, and long enough for their Mexican escorts to raise their rifles and fire shots toward the men on the bridge.

Arthur's horse reared and backed from the flash and the gunshots. Arthur grabbed for the saddle horn, but missed and was pitched out the saddle, off the bridge, and down the slippery sides of the rocky ravine. He hit hard, grabbing at mesquite bushes, scraping against chunks of shale. His poncho caught on a bush and stopped his fall just above the rushing water. He curled up, holding his side, his hat out of reach above him in the mud.

Flaherty jumped down as a bullet hit the log floor of the bridge. "Don't shoot, you stupid bastards," he yelled and waved his arms. He hit the ground with one hand holding the coil of rope hooked onto his saddle. He looped the rope onto a broken railing on the bridge, tossing the coil over the side toward Arthur, and slid down after it. Together, they untangled the Norwegian and pulled themselves up out of the mud and stopped at the edge of the canyon, peering at the tavern from behind a bush. In the light of the tavern door, Heinz and the other man in a black coat and homburg grabbed the two with rifles and pushed them inside. The door closed.

"That's *him* all right," Arthur said, sitting in the mud and rubbing his side. "The man I saw at Zork's loading cases, and again on our train."

"That was Heinz, too." Flaherty asked. "What's this all about?"

"I don't know," said Arthur. "but we're going to find out. We didn't sign up to be targets. Let's get our job done and back to El Paso."

Chapter Sixteen
Against the Wall

For once Flaherty met the sunrise with Arthur at the mine shack. They grunted and strained to pull parts together in a semblance of progress.

"About an inch now and the shaft will reach," said Arthur. They used six-foot pry bars to nudge the whole section of machinery, so that it would now fit with the too-short shaft from El Paso.

"Maybe even today, Flaherty," said Arthur, spitting on the ground. They struggled for several hours with the parts, bracing this and moving that. Tomás brought tortillas, beans, apples, and two beers. Arthur took the sledgehammer and forced in a wooden post to hold the gear casing in place. "If this kicks out, the whole thing will collapse," Arthur said. "So stand back, Flaherty—way back, and pray."

He connected the battery cables and turned the switch to heat the diesel glow-plugs. "Stand back more," he shouted, and he connected the starting switch wires.

Sparks flew, a loud explosion shook the shed, and the engine coughed and began to rattle away. Arthur wiped his eyes from the smoke and smiled.

He let the engine run for a few minutes. "Now," he shouted above the noise, wiping the fumes from his nose. Pulling a lever that connected the turning engine shaft to the assembly of gears and other parts, wheels and gears began to turn and squeal. With the machine working it could crush the gold ore—if a belt could be found to deliver the ore from the end of the rails out of the mountain.

"Holy blessed Virgin!" shouted Flaherty, throwing up his hands. "It's working!"

"Your prayer worked, Flaherty," said Arthur and slapped the Irishman on his shoulder.

"I forgot to pray," Flaherty said.

"It was my prayer then. He heard us just the same."

Applause now filled the room. Carlos the cook, Tomás and his grandfather, and Smythe were standing in the door of the shed.

"We did it!" Arthur threw his arm around the Irishman's shoulders and they stood together as if posing for the press.

"Is miracle," said the cook, waving away the smoke with his dishcloth.

"That ought to bring them back," said Smythe.

"I knew you would do it," said Tomás. "*Qué bueno!*"

"Bring who?" asked Arthur.

"Whoever first hears the sound," said Smythe, "the

Federáles or the Villistas. They both want the gold."

Arthur stiffened and snapped a look at the others. "Where's Heinz?" Arthur asked.

"Not know," said Carlos, "not come to breakfast."

"Flaherty, we have done our job," said Arthur. He smiled and pointed to the clatter and smoke. "Wonderful sound, ja?"

In the pass between the hills that contained the gold ore they wanted, twelve dirty white-uniformed men on horseback slouched in their saddles. A short sweating soldier panted and tripped up the steep road from the mine where he had been sent to hide, watch, and listen. "*Está trabajando la mina,*" he said, breathless, wiping his brow and saluting the officer. They shook their reins and spurred their horses at a walk down to the mine site and gathered behind the shed, the news of their arrival cloaked by the racket of the diesel engine. The leader, a man with a brown belt and a hat that resembled a visored pill-box, flicked his heels, and his horse shuffled forward a few feet into view of all in the machine shed.

"Good day. I am Colonel Herrera," the visitor shouted in broken English. "I now take control of the mine."

Arthur moved over and disconnected the wires and the engine coughed to a stop. The sudden silence was like a vacuum.

It was Arthur who first spoke. "What did you say,

Colonel?" Arthur looked the Federále officer in the eyes, then at his horse's hooves, then at his slouching men in their soiled uniforms. He was scared. He remembered what had happened to the Mexican mine crew Ayles failed to tell them was murdered by this officer.

"Do you understand what I say?" the officer repeated, looking at Arthur and Flaherty. "Do you gringos understand?" he said, spiting on the ground, and holding his gaze on them, demanding an answer, pulled his Colt from its holster.

Arthur met his look and answered with a sense of authority. "We are here to get the machinery running again. Then we will leave."

"You will leave when gold is coming from this mine, gringo."

"Colonel," spoke up Flaherty, "there is no belt to bring the ore to the mill."

"Then get the Indians to carry it on their backs as before," said Colonel Herrera.

"We don't know anything about that," said Flaherty.

"Then you are no longer needed here, are you? Your friend here," the Colonel said. "You, gringo!" pointing his pistol at Arthur. "Stand there, against that wall."

The cook, Tomás, and the grandfather backed around the corner of the shed.

Arthur didn't move.

"*No comprende*, gringo?" The Colonel's pistol roared and a spray of dirt kicked up at Arthur's feet. A rock splinter hit him in the cheek.

Arthur stumbled toward the wall of the shed, his eyes wide with surprise, wiping the blood from his face.

"Now, am I understood? I will be back tomorrow and this mill will be crushing gold ore or—" The pistol roared again, and the bullet hit the wall a foot over Arthur's head spraying him with broken adobe and dust.

"What is going on here?" a new voice shouted.

"Señor Heinz, *buenos dias*," the Colonel said to the German. "It looks like we will have our gold again."

"This is not necessary, Colonel," said Heinz. "You know that."

Colonel Herrera pointed his pistol at Arthur and Flaherty, the engine. "But—"

"These are good people here," Heinz said. "Take your men and leave, Colonel," he ordered. The authority in the German's voice shocked Arthur and Flaherty. It was a different Heinz. It was a military Heinz.

Flaherty, looking about for an answer, said in a stage whisper, "What the hell is going on here?"

Smythe was quick to respond. "Haven't you figured it out yet? Where do you think these Mexicans get so many guns, two or three on each horse, a Federále horse or a Villista horse it makes no difference? Where do you think, Irishman?"

Flaherty turned to Smythe with a look of disgust. He wanted an answer, but not from that insulting Englishman.

Smythe didn't stop. "American guns, German money.

Can't you see beyond your broken machine? With a war on its border, America is not yet in the European war, and Englishmen are dying. The salesman from El Paso, you must have seen him. Black suit and homburg?" Smythe waved his hands, shaping a hat. "German money for guns for both sides. Simple."

Arthur and Flaherty exchanged worried looks. They didn't have to say a thing. It all made sense now.

Colonel Herrera turned his horse and the Federáles followed to the grinding sound of hooves in the gravel and squeaking saddles. Heinz threw a cold look toward Smythe, turned and descended the hill without a word.

Arthur held up his hand. "Wait a minute, Mr. Heinz. What does all this have to do with the war in Europe? Last night, at the tavern, we were shot at. You were there—with the man in the suit."

"Yeah," said Flaherty. "You could have killed us."

Heinz stopped, turned, and hesitated. Then he said, "Sorry about that. They could have, but they didn't. If they wanted to hit you, you wouldn't be here now. That should answer your question. We had business to do, that's all. You were not a target." He turned to go, but cocked his head toward the Englishman and added, "Ask Mr. Smythe here if you want more, he knows everything." And he stepped down the hill.

"I know nothing about last night," said Smythe to the gringos. "None of this has anything to do with you, but you came here and walked into the middle of it. Who do you think Herr Heinz is? An engineer? Not hardly. He is an officer in the Kaiser's army."

Arthur wiped the blood off his face. "And who are you, Mr. Smythe?"

"I'm an Englishman."

Tomás arrived up the hill, stepped forward, and said, "It came this afternoon." He gave the letter to Arthur.

Chapter Seventeen
The Exit

It was three days since the visit of Colonel Herrera and his pistol. Arthur started up the engine every day, fooling everyone that the mill was working again, all except for the missing belt. His face cut was covered by a small bandage courtesy of Carlos.

"Is it Thursday, Flaherty?"

"That it is, my friend."

"Then he should be coming. His letter said Thursday."

The two sat side-by-side in the shade against the adobe wall of the shed. Arthur waved away a bee from his face, and Flaherty sipped his beer. They looked down the road toward the old church with its fresh grave of Rufus Abercrombie.

"What happened to Heinz?" Flaherty asked. "Haven't seen him since the Federáles' visit."

"I don't know. He eats at different times, and I saw him ride toward Parral," said Arthur. "But that is not our business."

"*Buenos tardes*, señores." Tomás settled in the dirt beside them. "Grandfather is sick," he said. "Ayles coming soon from Parral with another wagon. Everyone think you are saints. Fixing the machinery to run."

"It won't run for long, my friend," said Arthur. "Little fuel." He pointed to the empty barrels.

"When the war is over," Tomas said, "there will be fuel, and gold for the owners and pesos for all of us."

"This war," Flaherty said, "won't be over if the Germans keep selling guns to both sides. So is that what Heinz does?"

"Sí, *señor*, Heinz gives the orders to the man from El Paso. "He delivers the guns and bullets, and Heinz goes to telegraph and sends money to Zork, the same place you get your parts. But we are not supposed to know."

"The man at the tavern, Arthur," said Flaherty.

"I told you. He was on our train. Our cases had bad parts, his had good guns," said Arthur.

"The Parral newspaper," Tomás said. "It tells about the war in Europe. So many die. America won't go to war, it says. I read so I tell the others."

"The Yanks won't go to war if there's one here on its border," said Flaherty. "So that's what that sneaky Smythe is here for? To spy on Heinz for the English. A lot of good that'll do."

"Sí, señor. *Claro*. Smythe, he go to Parral to send telegrams, too."

"Well, Tomás, it isn't fair, is it?" said Arthur. "Guns and bullets, and no peace for you and your grandfather."

"First comes the guns, and then comes the peace," said Tomás.

"Not always," said Flaherty.

"Look!" Arthur pointed to a wagon rattling down the road toward them in a cloud of dust.

Arthur and Flaherty continued sitting in the dirt against the shed while Tomás ran to meet the wagon and guided Ayles up the hill. The easterner, in his wrinkled pin-striped suit, showed the fatigue of the trip.

"Well, gentlemen," Ayles said, "it seems you have accomplished your task."

"Ja, vell, Mr. Ayles," said Arthur, "no thanks to you and your wrong parts."

"The parts," said Ayles, "were ordered by the engineer, Mr. Johannesen."

"You mean the former manager Mr. Abercrombie?" asked Flaherty? "You passed his grave by the church." He pointed down the road.

"Perhaps so," said Ayles, and he looked into the shed. Arthur followed and touched the wires, the engine coughed, erupted, and clanked away with a convincing cloud of smoke. Ayles scratched his head and turned to look at Arthur and his assistant, the team he had hired to do exactly this, but never expected they would with wrong-sized parts. "You really did it. Quite amazing."

"It was easy," said Arthur, winking at Flaherty.

"Oh well, let's get on with it," said Ayles.

"The belt is missing," Arthur said.

"That won't matter, Mr. Johannesen," said Ayles.

Suitcases packed, they sat on their beds, awaiting Ayles. When he came to their room, he dragged in a bulging leather case with belts and ropes holding it closed. They pulled up the scarred table and the three chairs.

"Unless you have found a new home here…" and Ayles let out a big laugh, "…I assume you would like to go back to Texas now."

Arthur and Flaherty said nothing; their eyes on the case.

"So I am prepared to pay you. I brought pesos."

"You said we could have dollars, Ayles, and in the U.S. so we wouldn't be robbed," said Arthur.

"We prefer dollars, Mr. Ayles," Flaherty added, "the peso is worthless."

"You're right, Mr. Flaherty, but not entirely worthless. It's about thirty pesos to the dollar today."

Arthur spread his hands in disbelief. "It was ten when we left El Paso—ten cents a peso. That's three cents now?"

"Then," said Ayles, "you better hurry home before it's nothing."

"Better still we have dollars," said Flaherty. "Pesos will be worthless for the trip there."

"For that reason," Ayles said, "they may not kill you.

Take pesos. That's what I brought."

Ayles took out a knife and cut the ropes and unbuckled the straps. The case popped open and some bills fell on the floor The bills were soiled and wrinkled, some wrapped in tape, and all Arthur or Flaherty could read were the numbers: 10, 20, 50, 100.

"Here is what was promised," said Ayles, "plus a little more for your trip. You can count it if you wish."

"We would be here another week if we did that," Arthur said.

"Then trust me," said Ayles.

"Sure, like before. I have the expense and trip records you wanted," said Arthur and he reached for his notebook.

"That won't be necessary, Mr. Johannesen, I suggest you prepare your departure as soon as possible. That is a personal recommendation."

Ayles was ten feet out the door when they grabbed their suitcases and emptied most of their clothes on the beds. Then they packed in the pesos, not counting or dividing the money evenly. There was room in each case only for an extra pair of pants and a shirt, their razors and some soap. Flaherty kept the plaid pants for special times.

"Ready, señores?" Tomás stood in their doorway. "Grandfather is still sick, *muy malo*. I drive you myself. We go now. This morning the road to Parral is closed. Federáles. We go the back way to Jiménez for your train."

Carlos leaned in the door. "Good time meet you gentmin," he said and handed them a bundle he said contained food. "Food all cook. Fluit, too. Hope OK all way to Amelica, ha."

Smythe walked up with a sincere face without the smirk, and offered his hand to Arthur and turned to Flaherty. "No hard feelings, ole boy," he said. "I hope you make it back to Texas safely. We will all be in this together soon—and a long way from here."

"Thanks, Smythe." Flaherty flashed a quick smile and nodded. "Perhaps we will."

They jumped into the waiting wagon with their bulging suitcases, and Tomás took them down a different path out of La Promesa, one they had not seen before, down the hill on the east side. There, on a horse waiting for them at the opened gate, was Heinz.

"Well," Arthur looked around, "we're glad you're alone this time, Heinz."

"My apologies, gentlemen, really," said Heinz. "It was a private meeting at the cantina and the men were instructed to scare off anyone. We didn't know it was you at first."

"Well scare us it did," said Flaherty.

"Heinz, we were just passing by that night." Arthur knotted his brow, and raised his arms. "Do you think guns do all the talking? Try words next time."

Heinz had no further response to the shooting, only the future. "I will say it again. I didn't start this war. You are right, Mr. Johannesen. Words are preferable. If I were not here, I would be in France, maybe dead like my school-mates. Just as many Germans died in that same battle, and it isn't over yet. You had better hope you don't go to France. Who is to know?"

"Well, Heinz," said Arthur, "we hope to first get out of this Mexican war. One war at a time."

"You are in good hands." Heinz nodded toward Tomás and warned, "Keep to the river road toward Allende and keep your eyes open."

A thundering crash came from the direction of the mine. A plume of black smoke and dust curled up the hillside.

"What is *that*!" Arthur said.

"That will be the work of Mr. Ayles," Heinz said. "Doing what he is paid to do. The owner of course does not want the gold to go to anyone but himself when it's all over."

Arthur shook his hands in the air. "And for this stupid man we risked our lives?" He turned and spit on the ground.

"The owner," said Heinz, "wants to make a show of fixing the mine, with outside mechanics like you, hoping the army or Villa won't take it over. But he won't be able to fool them much longer."

"Let's go, Johannesen," Flaherty said, patting Arthur on the shoulder.

Heinz added, "The whole thing is delaying the inevitable. In the end the mine will be taken by one side or the other, and America will be fighting against my country in Europe. It is all for nothing."

"We did make it run, for a while," said Arthur. "That job was accomplished."

"It'll all be over soon, I hope," said Heinz. "Have a safe trip home." He saluted them.

Chapter Eighteen
Hotel Centrál

The horses strained, but the trail was too steep, so the passengers got off the loaded wagon and helped push it through the narrow pass. Then it was all downhill. They passed south of Sombreretillo and connected with the river road west of Allende. At dusk they pulled off the trail, well out of sight for the night, into a scrub of piñon pines, oaks, and junipers.

"No fire tonight, señores," said Tomás. They opened the food bag from Carlos, cold tortillas and cooked meat. There were no complaints as they unrolled the bedrolls and crawled in. "Señores," said Tomás, "soon the war will be over, and you will come back to Mexico I hope."

Arthur, Flaherty, and Tomás lay there, silent, looking at the stars, breathing in the juniper, and slapping the mosquitoes.

"We need good men in this country," said Tomás, "like you."

"*You* are a good man," Arthur said. "Take care of yourself and your grandfather. You'll see the end of this bloody thing and a new and happy life. Be patient and stay out of the shooting."

"Guns," said Flaherty, "are needed at times, my friend, but when the men are big enough to put away the guns and talk out their problems, then you will have a country. And you won't need the gringos or anyone else."

"Listen to Flaherty, Tomás," said Arthur. "Guns are only to kill. Dead men don't make a nation. You are a smart man. So stay alive. Serve your country with good and brave ideas."

"And now, señores? What about you?"

"Johannesen here," said Flaherty, "he has a pretty girlfriend waiting for him in El Paso. And a job, he tells me. For me, who knows?"

"Maybe only a few more days," Arthur said. "You see those stars there?"

Tomás gazed into the dark, "Sí, the Big Dipper."

"And see where those two stars point?"

"Sí, Polaris."

"That is where we're heading, north," said Arthur. "She is the prettiest, sweetest thing you can imagine. Sometimes I thought I might not see her again. But, here we are. And next, if she is waiting, a family, a good job. That's all I want."

"But you, señor?" Tomás turned to the Irishman.

"I have no idea, my friend. Something will come along.

The Irish are a lucky clan, you know."

They slept the best they could on the rocky ground.

The next morning Tomás awoke with a shock to the sounds of men and horses somewhere in the distance. He crawled over the rise toward the noise, the tangled underbrush scratching his face. He found that if they had gone any further into the woods the night before, they would be sleeping with the Federáles. Through the dirt and twigs, he saw twenty white tents beside the crumbling walls of a hacienda. Cavalrymen in white uniforms were racing their horses up and down and yelling.

Tomás backed down and put his finger to his lips. "Señores, fold up everything. *Pronto*. We leave now." Tomás harnessed the horses, hoping a noisy horse would not announce their presence. He decided to take a road around Allende, not knowing who was in command of the town. Tomás demanded the most out of the horses and didn't stop for lunch or rest. They didn't see Federáles again, until they got to the houses on the edge of Jiménez at dusk, and then they were dead Federáles, lying in the streets, without guns or boots.

Tomás made a quick reconnaissance and reported, "Much fighting all night. Maybe town in control of Federáles, maybe not."

Jimenez was a different town from when they left it three weeks before. They passed the bodies of government soldiers along the road, some stripped of their jackets and pants.

"Hotel Centrál, señores, is where I take you."

Shouting police commanded the collection of bodies which were dumped into wagons like bags of garbage.

"Their pockets have already been cleaned by the police for sure," said Tomás.

Arthur, having never seen the horrors of war before and the inhumanity, absorbed all this soberly. He pushed along, hoping to see the dead no more.

The Hotel Centrál was identified by the faded white letters two feet high sprawled across a splintered wooden sign hanging from its broken balcony. Bullets had left one window shattered and holes on the faded outside walls that were once blue. Inside, the wooden lobby smelled of emptiness and their boots echoed across the planked floor.

"Welcome to Hotel Centrál," a happy voice greeted them with a smile and good English. "I am Florence Townes, the proprietress of this establishment. My middle name is Margaret. Call me Margarita. I hope the shooting is over for the night."

"You are American?" asked Arthur.

"I'm what they call a 'railroad widow,'" she said. Her hair, once blond, was graying, uncombed, and fell off her shoulders, but she had a nice smile. "I'm from Kansas City. My husband was a founder of the *Ferrocarril Centrál*."

Her horn-rimmed glasses perched on her nose, and she looked up at her customers and down on the desk without moving her head. She was in her late thirties, maybe older, and wore a calico dress.

"Richard disappeared four years ago. I still run the hotel." With a rag she wiped off the counter and moved the guest book forward for them to sign. "You will be safe here, I think. Dinner is at eight."

Arthur pushed forward a wad of pesos from which Mrs. Townes counted out some, pushed back the balance, and assured them of the correct fare of twenty pesos each for the night.

Arthur turned to Tomás. "Will you stay here tonight? You can return home in the morning."

"No, señores, I have cousin outside of town. I say goodbye now." He took his hat in his hand. "My horses will not be safe here."

Arthur and Flaherty both felt a pang of respect and of fear for this young man—so hopeful, determined, so in tune with the ideals of the revolution. He had saved their lives more than once. They each hugged Tomás, and Arthur stuffed pesos in both pockets of the young Mexican's baggy white trousers.

"Remember, Tomás," said Arthur, "it's good ideas and hard work that finally will win the peace." Arthur had admired Tomás' dedication and commitment from the start, and even more so now. "Stay alive so you can put your good ideas to work for your family and your country."

Flaherty put his arm on the young man's shoulder. "It won't be easy, my friend. Remember what I said. Keep the faith. You will have your success. I know." The young Mexican and the Irishman embraced again, and Tomás turned, left the hotel, climbed up onto the wagon, snapped his reins, and drove away, waving back once.

"May we have the room key, Mrs. Townes?" asked Arthur.

"Room 27. No key, gentlemen." She waved her hand. "You'll find the lock is shot off." She stepped out from behind the desk and leaned closer to Arthur, saying in a whisper. "And you'll be smart if you leave your suitcases un-locked. That way," she said, "if you're robbed, they will take what they want, then leave and not cut your throat."

Arthur turned to his partner. "Did you hear that, Flaherty? We are in a safe place."

"But," added Mrs. Townes, "we haven't had a robbery here for weeks."

Chapter Nineteen
Room 27

Cantina Alegre was only three blocks away from the hotel. The cantina's heavy oak doors were splintered from bullets passing through, some going in and some going out. Arthur and Flaherty took two seats farthest from the door, they being the first customers of the day and remembering that Mrs. Townes warned they should stay out of sight and away from windows and doors. Two warm beers were placed in front of them. The Federáles had lost many soldiers, Mrs. Townes had said, but some were still in town, and Villa's forces were roaming the streets in search of them.

They sat in silence, focusing on their beer, not wanting to draw attention by their language, but that didn't work. "Good morning, amigos," the bartender said in English. "Are you coming or going?"

"We are waiting for the train north," said Arthur, glancing at the door.

"*Bueno!* I may see you here for a while, amigos," the bartender said.

The door opened and shadows passed across the outdoor glare as two men entered. The Federále soldiers, who in their once-white uniforms, had cringed behind walls, crawled in the dirt, and soaked in their sweat for days, nevertheless sat on the stools and greeted the bartender as if they were expected.

"We will check on the train today, we will," said Flaherty. The door opened again and four soldiers joined the others at the far end of the bar. The bartender ran his rag along the bar top as he strolled down to serve the soldiers their morning beers.

"Looks like we won't be alone," Arthur whispered to his partner. The door stood open now and more soldiers filed in, slapping backs, laughing, and leaning their rifles against the bar.

Flaherty looked past Arthur, searching for a back door should a quick exit be needed, but saw none.

More soldiers filed in, taking up all the bar stools right up against Flaherty and leaving several men standing between the others. The soldier next to Flaherty nodded a greeting, and through a ragged mustache and rotting teeth, hissed a "Buenos dias," then turned away to talk to his buddy. Flaherty turned to Arthur and wrinkled his nose.

Arthur and Flaherty were served their second beers after all the soldiers had theirs. One of the soldiers down the line leaned over and whispered to the bartender something which made the others look towards the foreigners. The soldiers nodded their heads and smiled under their bushy mustaches, raising their glasses in a toast. Arthur and Flaherty nodded and faked smiles, knowing it was the right thing to do but not knowing why. The bartender slid his rag along the bar toward them.

"The sergeant," said the bartender, "he says he and his men thank you for your generosity." He wiped the bar. "After the next beer," he said, "they will have to report for duty and can't stay longer."

"Just pay and don't argue," said Flaherty.

"Did you think I would argue?" said Arthur. "I didn't know life was so cheap." The bill was 125 pesos, at that day's rate of exchange about four dollars. They paid up fast.

"Flaherty," Arthur said, "find us a smaller bar, the smallest in town."

The visit to the train station resulted only in shrugs, even from the stationmaster they had known before. He told them he expected a train when he saw one coming down the tracks. As far as he knew, the tracks were blocked by Villa.

At *Tío Pepe's*, they found a bar with only six stools and camped there the rest of the day. The bartender was friendly and seemed to understand their plight. He served them a chili soup that raised sweat beads on their foreheads. It was then they heard the sounds of cannon.

"Fighting again?" Arthur asked.

The bartender didn't understand, so Flaherty said, "Boom boom," pointing towards the sound.

"*Si, Villa anoche,*" the bartender said, "*soldados se vey.*" He cartooned running soldiers across the bar with his fingers, then wiped his glasses and the mirror. "*Espero que sí,*" he said. He kept feeding them *piñon* nuts and hard tortilla chips. The booming cannon and popping rifles sounded in the distance.

Arthur pulled out his pocket watch and saw it read after four. "No siesta today, Flaherty."

The door opened and a senorita danced into the room, flashing her red and gold flowered skirt at the foreigners.

"*Muy bonita, muy bonita,*" the bartender said, raising his eyebrows toward the girl, reaching for her hand and kissing it. She slid onto the stool next to Flaherty. The display from the low cut square in her white blouse and her smiling brown eyes melted the Irishman. They were not the normal brown eyes, but had a tint of green in them which reminded the Irishman of home. While her attention was focused on Flaherty, Arthur, his head facing his beer, didn't miss much out the corners of his eyes. He licked his lips.

The bartender served her a warm soft drink in a glass bottle. "*Somos la unica cantina en Jiménez que tiene Coca-Cola,*" he said with pride. "*Tenemos amigos en El Paso.*"

"Don't brag, Tío," she said, "others will find you out."

"Luisa, she dances like the bird," the bartender said. "She speaks the English bueno."

"Everyone calls him *Tío,*" she said, "but he is not really

anyone's uncle, but everyone's friend."

A tall man with a guitar case and a black sombrero with a silver band entered the small room. The foreigners were on their third beer when he started to play. Luisa wrapped a wool shawl about her shoulders and started to dance. Her skirt swirled and her heels clicked. They were the only ones in this bar with only three tables. The entertainment ended abruptly.

"Señores," the bartender said, "I am sorry, but no one comes to Tío Pepe's tonight. Afraid of guns. I close now." Outside they found Tio Pepe correct. The darkening streets were empty except for small groups of soldiers, all fleeing in the same direction, dragging their rifles and losing their caps. Luisa found the company of the foreigners a comfort, and the three of them rushed through the shadows to the Hotel Centrál. It was shuttered and dark, but the door opened to Arthur's knock. Inside the light of kerosene lamps threw long shadows. Arthur found himself suddenly alone. "They," Mrs. Townes motioned her pen toward the stairs as Flaherty and Luisa vanished, "want to be private I think."

Arthur removed his hat. "We have to check the train early tomorrow."

"Tomorrow is tomorrow, Mr. Johannesen," Mrs. Townes said and motioned him to the dark sitting room with two over-stuffed chairs, a sofa leaking its insides, and an end table with a burning candle dripping its wax down the sides of a tequila bottle.

"May I call you Arthur?" she said. She motioned him to

sit on the sofa. Over the sofa on the red papered wall was a framed poster of a train exiting a tunnel.

"It's from France," she said. "Do you like it?" She sat down by Arthur, her hip touching his. "You may call me Margarita." She produced a bottle of wine, two glasses, and a small bottle of medicinal alcohol. "Here," she said and tenderly removed the dirty bandage from his face, made a grimace at his cut, washed it with the alcohol and applied a clean bandage.

"Ja, of course, very nice. Thank you." Arthur moved to the end of the sofa, against the arm.

"I have been here on my own for four years now," she said as she poured the wine. "Richard disappeared in 1912. Never a word. It is nice to have some American guests."

"I'm from Norway."

"All the same."

Mrs. Townes was in a skirt and a revealing white blouse like the dancing señoritas wear, and there was plenty she was rightly proud of in spite of a few wrinkles in her tanned skin. The hard-working proprietress of the Hotel Centrál was a good ten years older than Arthur, but that, Arthur realized, posed no problem to her.

"Better than these arrogant Mexican politicians and dirty rebels," she said. "Except for 'The Hawk,' of course. He is a deadly man, they say, but he is always polite to me and stays here often. He even picks up his towels."

"Are we under room 27?" Arthur asked. The knocks and banging from overhead was increasing and rhythmic, not to be confused with the sporadic cannon gunfire somewhere outside.

"Yes," she said and moved closer and put her hand on his leg. "We can have dinner afterward."

Arthur's glances bounced between the dripping candle and the approaching woman. By the third glass of wine, Arthur was not complaining and well cornered in the sofa under Mrs. Townes' persistence. Her blouse fell off one shoulder. She ran her fingers through his hair, and for a moment he remembered how Pauline did the same on the park bench in El Paso. Her fingers began to unbutton his shirt and his hand found itself on her bare leg as he leaned closer. The other shoulder of her blouse dropped, and he focused on the flesh emerging from under that embroidered whiteness.

She continued to slip off his shirt, then reached for his belt buckle, loosened it, and pulled out his shirttail and slipped the shirt off his shoulders. His shirt dropped on the floor and out the pocket popped open the golden heart-shaped frame-with the smiling eyes of Pauline waiting for him in Texas.

"Oh, my God," said Arthur, and he pulled back.

"It's only tonight, Arthur." She pulled him back.

"Sorry," he said, and straightened up.

"We'll wait on Mr. Flaherty and Luisa," Mrs. Townes said as she busied herself in the kitchen. Arthur sat waiting at the table set for four, as he had for an hour. It was past nine when Flaherty and Luisa joined them.

"Ja, vell," said Arthur, "I bet you are hungry."

They smiled.

"The fighting seems to be dying out," said Luisa.

"You think so?" said Arthur without a smile. "Mrs. Townes has pea soup and chicken."

Now and then cannon fire and gun shots still rattled the windows from somewhere on the edge of town.

"Do you know," said Flaherty, "that Luisa's uncle is a commander with Pancho Villa?"

"Then we should see him tomorrow," said Mrs. Townes, entering with a big bowl of pea soup in her hands. "Villa should take Jiménez tonight. The Federáles have run, so we may have some quiet." She put a large porcelain ladle into the soup and returned to the kitchen.

"And listen to this," Flaherty added, "his name is Marcus Aurelius. Marcus Aurelius Zamora it is. What a fine name for a warrior for justice and equality and peace."

Arthur ladled the soup into his bowl as Mrs. Townes entered with a platter of steaming chicken. "He has stayed here, her uncle has," added Mrs. Townes. "And he signs his full name, not just 'El Halcón—The Hawk.'"

A shock, like electricity, went through the Irishman's body, he looked at Arthur who stopped his ladle of soup half way to his bowl, spilling it on the fresh table cloth.

Flaherty turned to Luisa and said. "Your uncle, Marcus Aurelius, is 'The Hawk'?"

"Yes, but we keep it quiet," Luisa said. "Those soldiers

do terrible things. My father is gone. Uncle Marcus is my only protector."

Flaherty looked at his chicken and said, "Holy Mother of God."

"Good," said Mrs. Townes, "now that Mr. Flaherty has said Grace—we can eat."

Chapter Twenty
Holy Refuge

The Captain stood over six feet tall, in a clean khaki shirt, his pants folded into brown boots. He was poised at attention before Mrs. Townes. Captain Orozco carried only a Mauser pistol in a beaded leather hip holster. "Señora Margarita," said Captain Orozco, "we know she went home this morning, but she was here all night and seen with the red-headed gringo in the evening. Now what do we report to our leader?" The Villista turned to his soldiers, all grinning through their mustaches and nodding to each other.

"I told you, Captain, she stayed in the special room I keep for her uncle," Mrs. Townes said, and that was the truth. "She was safe all night," she added.

"Where are the gringos now?" the captain asked, his eyes flashing up the stairs.

"My guests were very nice men," she said. "Gentlemen." That was the truth she wanted them to hear.

"And now?" he insisted.

"They left after breakfast," she lied.

"I will take your word, Señora Margarita, but we will find them and ask the questions ourselves. Those are my orders. You know how close her uncle is to *la sobrina*. He protects her like a hawk protects it's chick."

A sharp clink was heard from somewhere above as something hit the floor. The Captain started for the stairs.

Mrs. Townes stopped him with a firm hand. "Consuelo is cleaning," she said, and that was a lie, too.

The captain dipped his head imitating respect, and as The Hawk's men were leaving, Mrs. Townes stomped up the stairs calling, "Consuelo, we must finish by ten."

Flaherty and Arthur locked their suitcases, and the Irishman kneeled to retrieve his dropped pocket knife that had slid under the bed. They peeked around the corner to greet Mrs. Townes. "I think you saved our lives, Mrs. Townes," said Arthur.

"Margarita," she corrected him. "Mr. Flaherty, that girl Luisa likes you. I can tell."

"Quite special, she is. Intelligent, speaks English, and—" he cleared his throat, "—very nice. But I like being single— it's freedom."

Mrs. Townes smiled, looking at Arthur over the top of her glasses.

Lifting his arms, Flaherty said, "So what do we do now?"

"Sorry, gentlemen, you can't stay here," she said. "The Captain and his troops will come back. The Hawk is very protective of his family."

"Oh my God!" Flaherty said. Hanging his head, he looked at Arthur out the corner of his eyes.

"That's the answer. Thank you, Flaherty," snapped Arthur.

"What do you mean?" said the Irishman.

"God," he said, "The Virgin Mary, I knew a Catholic would be helpful."

"What are you talking about?" she said.

"The nuns, where are the nuns?" Arthur said.

"The Convent of the Blessed Virgin?" she asked. "What do you know about that?"

"Roast beef, Margarita. Roast beef and green chilies."

Chapter Twenty-one
Pesos to the Wind

"Another time, my friends, another time." Mrs. Townes hugged them both, whispered, "Next time," in Arthur's ear, and pushed them out a back door with directions to the convent a long mile away. "Come back," she said looking directly at Arthur. Arthur hesitated just a moment, self-assured that Pauline's unexpected interruption of the couch party last night was a fortunate reminder of his honorable intentions back in El Paso.

They raced down the narrow alley between the wooden frame backsides of stores and cafés to the wide street, wrestling their peso-filled suitcases and turning left as instructed, then slowed to a walk as to not attract attention. But a soldier of the Captain's band had been assigned to each street corner near the hotel. The soldier shouted the alarm, shook his rifle in the air, and his compatriots all came running, grabbing their rifles and hats and stumbling after the foreigners.

"My God, run!" Arthur yelled. Flaherty was already steps ahead of the Norwegian.

"Pare! Pare!" the soldiers yelled at the foreigners, holding onto their sombreros with one hand and their rifles with the other.

But the Norwegian and Irishman ran faster, lugging their suitcases of pesos. "What did she say?" Flaherty wheezed, "By the fruit market, right or left?"

"Right," called Arthur turning in that direction.

"No, left, by the red fence, she said," yelled Flaherty.

"No, right," and Arthur slowed, looking back at the soldiers gaining amidst their indecision.

"Right, right," called Flaherty, and as he turned to catch up with his partner, his suitcase slammed onto a post of the red fence, jamming open the locks, pesos flying through the air like a frightened flock of doves. Flaherty grabbed the case shut again and ran on.

Out of breath, the poor Villistas slowed, looked both ways and back to confirm the captain had not followed them, and started scavenging the peso bills, like hungry squirrels after a picnic.

Flaherty pulled hard on the bell rope at the convent wall, looking back, but their pursuers were nowhere in sight. The door, big enough for a truck, was unlatched, and he pushed it open to see a bent old lady in black shuffling toward them.

"Good day, my sons," she said. "Welcome to Convent of the Blessed Virgin."

"Good morning, Sister," said Flaherty in his most reverent voice and crossing himself.

"May I know your business, please? Visiting days are Wednesdays and Fridays."

"Dear Sister," said the Irishman, "we have come on matters of utmost importance, and wish to see Sisters Elizabeth and Mercedes."

"What's that?" the nun cocked her head and inched closer with a hand behind her ear.

"Sisters Elizabeth and Mercedes, please," he shouted.

"Sister Elizabeth and Sister Mercedes? Yes, they are in this convent. It is Terce now."

"Yes, Sister, when can we meet Sisters Elizabeth and Mercedes?"

"Terce now, later the Sisters gather for their Obediences. Then some will go shopping, some gardening. You should come back on Wednesday."

"Speak louder, Flaherty," said Arthur, impatient. "Tell her it is a family emergency or something. So they know we are here."

The Sister scowled at the Norwegian. "Follow me, my sons," the Sister said. "You must talk to Father Ruiz. Later it will be Sext."

They followed the nun through the fragrance of a small well-kept garden of azaleas and roses. The adobe walls showed their age, the stucco fallen away in places. They met the priest, a gray-bearded man, on the way to the chapel across the central patio. He nodded his balding head in understanding when the Sister repeated their urgency.

"I am Father Ruiz. Welcome. This is a Franciscan convent. You are always welcome." He took a long look at the two foreigners, called to a novitiate, and sent her running. Soon Sister Elizabeth, the one with the big eyebrows, came hurrying out of the washroom, wiping her hands on a rag and smiling.

"Ah, what a nice surprise, our *Norteño* friends," she said, smoothing the white apron tied across her habit.

Sister Mercedes came running down the corridor of adobe cells, greeting them like family, and the priest, the two nuns, the Catholic Irishman and the Lutheran Norwegian, sat on the concrete benches by the central fountain under the willow trees, and Flaherty explained their problem. They were offered sanctuary for as long as needed. Arthur replied, "We appreciate that and will pay for our keep, but we have to get back to El Paso as soon as possible, on the next train north."

"Nothing can be foretold in these times," said Father Ruiz. He had a natural smile and wisdom in his eyes. "There have been no trains north or south in days. But we will do our best." He crossed himself and joined his hands as in prayer.

The priest pulled the sisters aside for a word, then Sister Mercedes headed for the entry door, which was still standing half open, and disappeared toward the Jimenez rail station.

Chapter Twenty-two
The Saviors

The two gringos were given "guest quarters" within the walls of the Convent of the Blessed Virgin near the cell of Father Ruiz. Each room was about ten feet square, with a cot, a brown blanket, and a gray pillow. In the corner stood a small table with a wash pan and jug of water, the walls bare except for an imposing crucifix with a suffering Jesus. They ate on a small table in the adjoining main room, often with Father Ruiz, who they learned to respect.

Early the third day of their sanctuary, a boy of about twelve ran breathless into the convent, squeezing through the heavy doors, and told the first nun that he met he wanted to see Sister Mercedes. When the Sister appeared, she received his message, gave him a blessing and two pesos, and ran to find Father Ruiz.

"In an hour, maybe two, the only train to get through the blockade," she said to the Father. "Express to Juarez, important people on board. Soldiers, too. The Stationmaster said now is the time."

Just after Obediences, the heavy door pushed open and, as usual at that hour, the black cloaked nuns exited, two-by-two into the city. Jiménez was now comfortably under the control of The Hawk and his regiment of the Northern Army of the Revolution. The Hawk had taken the major part of his soldiers west to take the city of Hidalgo del Parral. The few men left behind had nothing to do, but watch the convent in case two foreigners within those high walls might decide to check out.

Lying about, smoking, and talking, the Villistas welcomed the exiting nuns, who smiled and blessed them and fed them fresh fruit from the convent's gardens and orchards. The rebels, their backs to the convent door, gathered around the nuns, their mouths full of a pear, apple, or orange. They did not see the departure of four veiled nuns, the two taller ones with baskets of fruit, and the shorter two struggling with battered leather suitcases. The exiting nuns turned away and strolled toward the city center where the station master had been paid two hundred of Arthur's pesos for news that a train was expected.

The bullet-scarred big engine of the *Ferrocarril Nacional* braked into the east side of the station, screaming like a dragon in pain, flooding the platform with steam and dripping water. The conductor jumped onto the ground, shouting they would stop for only ten minutes.

Around the corner and shielded from curious eyes by Sisters Elizabeth and Mercedes, Arthur and Flaherty slipped out of their clerical disguises, handed the borrowed habits to the Sisters, and relieved them of the suitcases. Arthur put food into a cloth bag. Flaherty crossed himself.

"God bless you and keep you," offered Sister Elizabeth. Sister Mercedes repeated the blessing, and the two men boarded the second of two passenger cars, the first being full of Federáles who, hatless and hiding their guns, peeked from behind pulled shades, unsure who was in control of Jiménez. The following two cars were red-slatted cattle cars with moaning black cows. A man in a blue suit and tie, his well-dressed wife and two teenaged daughters also boarded. There was six already there at the other end of the car, sitting is a special compartment, the curtains pulled.

"No other passengers?" Flaherty asked.

"The man in the suit looks important," whispered Arthur.

"And who knows who is in that curtained compartment?" said Flaherty. Everyone sat in silence while the nervous conductor ran back and forth outside, patting the cars as in blessing. Thirty minutes later, not ten, the boilers re-filled with water and the coal car with coal, the train jerked north.

At the same time on the west side of the Jimenez station, *The Express del Hidalgo del Parral* wheezed to a stop, dirty and stained from days of neglect, but the "76" on its cab still proudly visible. From its three cars and four flatbeds with side stakes, jumped out The Hawk and his victorious band of Villistas, returned from taking Parral.

Chapter Twenty-three
The Hawk Attacks

The Hawk, exhausted from three days of fighting, removed his boots, and reclined in the swivel chair in the City Hall office he had commandeered. "We only lost thirty men," he said. "But they were good men. I am not happy with that."

"But, Colonel, you have taken Parral," Captain Orozco said. "Now we support General Villa to take Chihuahua?"

"Captain," The Hawk said, "where is the red-headed gringo?"

"They got away, Colonel."

The Hawk stood up straight in his stocking feet. "What?" *Está imposíble!* How could such strange looking men get away in this small town?" He pulled on his boots. "That was my niece he forced himself on!" He grabbed his hat and raced to the door. "Find out where they went, *now*."

The Captain offered no excuse, but said, "We know

where they went, Colonel. They left on today's train to Ciudad Chihuahua."

The Colonel stopped, turned, and said, "*What* train! I thought they were all blocked."

"Not this one. It carried Don Emilio Carranza and a car of Federáles. We just now learned that from our boy at the station."

"*Que carai!* The President's brother? How can this be? Heading for El Paso?"

"With his cattle. We only had a handful of soldiers," said the Captain with his palms up in explanation.

The Hawk headed for the door again and called back. "They will never make it! I want the ten best shooters! At the station. *Now!*"

At the station there was only one train. Conductor Rodriguez, with a rag in his hand, was supervising the cleaning of the tall stack with its bright brass ring, and the polishing of the silver script number "76" painted on the side of its cab.

"Rodriguez!" the Hawk called. "Fire up again, we are going to El Paso!"

"*El Paso*, Colonel?" The conductor, his gold braided blue uniform disheveled and sweat-stained, stood, his mouth open in disbelief.

"One car only. Hurry," commanded The Hawk.

"But, Colonel—"

"Hurry!" The Hawk said. "You'll be surprised how fast your shiny lady will run. We have to catch another train."

"We are out of coal and water now," the engineer said.

"Disconnect those other cars, Rodriquez!"

"This is the *Express de Hidalgo del Parral*, Colonel, not *de El Paso*," Rodriguez protested.

"Uncle," Luisa called, running up in her short skirt and sandals, "I'm coming with you."

"Are you are crazy? This is no place for a woman. There will be shooting."

"How exciting," she said. "Uncle Marcus, pleeeese." And she smiled, cocked her head, and flashed her greenish eyes.

"No!" he said and turned away. "We'll be back tonight, or tomorrow, with your red-headed gringo."

The Norwegian and the Irishman sat quietly in the car at the other end from the Mexican President's brother. Only seventy miles out of Jiménez the train began to slow. Don Emilio, looking from side to side out the windows, gave a word to one of his officers, who rushed forward to learn the reason.

They stopped at *Delicias*, and the man with the family across the aisle explained the engine was low on water again, and they had to fill once more if they were to by-pass Ciudad Chihuahua due to the fighting reported there. "Besides," the man said, "there are leaks in the boiler from bullet holes."

"Oh," said Flaherty, and they sank back in the cushioned

seats. "Just so long as we make it. It's not in our hands, now."

Arthur nodded his agreement. "Ja, just keep heading north, that's all I ask. I have a date."

They rattled through Ciudad Chihuahua, carts and people scattering, and north onto the desert plain toward Texas, only a little over two hundred miles away.

"Did you ever think, Flaherty, that maybe we might not see the United States again?"

"Or Ireland, and at times if I would ever see daylight again."

"Me, too. Maybe never see Pauline again. Well, we are almost home now. Sometimes, I think I am too determined. Pig headed, that is what some have said. What good did it do to fix that mess of broken parts?"

"Yes, my friend I would say you are dogged."

"Dogged? What does that mean?"

"Like a dog on a pant leg. Doesn't give up when maybe he should. But don't complain. You have some dollars in the bank."

Chapter Twenty-four
The Chase

Engine 76, pulling one car with six soldiers, steamed out of Jimenez leaving a cloud of swirling black smoke in its wake. "Maybe," said Rodriquez, "we'll catch them in Ciudad Chihuahua."

"They have three hours head start. How fast can this beauty of yours go?"

"Fifty miles an hour, Colonel, but I have never asked her to do that. She is old."

"We'll catch them," The Hawk said. "They'll have to stop for water. The stationmaster said their boiler was leaking."

Shoveling coal into the firebox, the shirtless fireman, drenched in sweat, cast an insulting look at the Colonel and Rodriquez as they leaned out both sides looking for a train ahead.

"Ask for her best now, and we will always be friends," said The Hawk. "The Jimenez Station Master telegraphed ahead to let us pass through all stations including Chihuahua.

How far without refueling?"

"Only to Parral and back, Colonel. About the same as to Chihuahua one way."

The fireman leaned on his shovel and nervously looked at the boiler pressure gauge approaching the red line. Rodriquez nodded, and the fireman kept shoveling. The driver kept one hand on the regulator to control the speed and the other on the rope which rang the big copper bell to warn man and beast of engine 76's resolve. They sped through Delicias as if it wasn't there.

Approaching the city of Chihuahua, the driver pointed out that the water level was dangerously low.

"Colonel," said Rodriquez, "We have not seen them yet, and we won't if we run out of water in the desert."

"How long?"

"Thirty, forty minutes. It is difficult when hot."

Pulling onto a side track in Chihuahua, the fireman and helpers jumped on the hot engine, swearing at their burns. They pulled down the canvas tube from the water tank and let it flow. "Full to the very top!" called Rodriquez. In twenty minutes they were off again. They learned from workers a train that didn't stop had passed though two hours before.

The Colonel went back into the coach to ready his troops for action. He found them in a circle at the rear of the coach, their hats back, laughing with a woman. It was Luisa. He took one look, slapped his head with his fist, and said to himself, *What can I do with this girl? She will get us all in trouble*. And he returned to the cab to look for his target.

An hour out of Chihuahua, Arthur and Flaherty, their heads nodding to the rhythm of the rails, were happy that they would be back in El Paso before sundown.

"I sure hope she has waited," said Arthur.

"Your girlfriend?" said the Irishman, "Why shouldn't she wait? You are rich now." He laughed.

"It's been over two weeks."

"She should love you," said Flaherty. "You are a hero."

They didn't notice the train slowing. But, Don Emilio did, and he sent an officer forward again to find the reason.

"Just desert and barren hills," said Arthur looking out the window. The train kept slowing.

"There's a big bridge and a canyon," said the older girl across the aisle, a teenager in a blue jumper with a red crest from her Catholic school.

The squeal of the brakes now alarmed Flaherty. "Why are we stopping?"

"Look!" Arthur's face was plastered to the windows. "It's the crew! Look!" He turned to Flaherty. "They're running for that hill."

Don Emilio's officers ran to the car ahead, shouting. The soldiers poured out onto the desert with their guns, yelling, shooting in the air, spreading out, chasing the crew. Flaherty, Arthur, the family, all ran out onto the hot alkaline shell of an ancient lake bed.

With their fists and the butts of their rifles, the soldiers prodded the protesting crew members. "The crewmen say the engine is out of water again," the father said, "and the bridge ahead is mined to blow up. They refuse to go."

"The canyon," called Don Emilio. "Get buckets; there may be water in the bottom of the canyon."

A dozen canvas buckets were thrown to the men. A line of crew, soldiers, and passengers, descended the steep banks under the bridge to the pools of cool water amongst the salt-cedar and stunted oak on the rocky canyon floor. Arthur and Flaherty ended up on the bottom. The President's brother helped with advice, folding his arms, and staying on top, close to his car. No one wasted breath on talk. For an hour, they passed the empties down and the heavies up.

A crewman on the top of the engine poured the water into the boiler, and then he stopped. Holding an empty bucket in one hand and pointing to the horizon with the other, where the tracks from the south melted into the desert haze, he cried, "Look, another train coming!"

The conductor dropped his bucket and climbed on top and shouted down the line. "Hurry, everyone in the train!"

Soldiers and passengers scurried up the canyon sides, slipping in the loose shale, grabbing onto bushes for help, dropping buckets, and running to the train where the crew began firing up the engine, shoveling coal and pulling levers. Passengers raced for the cars. The growing cloud of black smoke curling down from the edge of the horizon filled everyone with the urgency to move.

"The bridge will blow up," someone yelled, but the big engine started to shake forward, steam curling from between the wheels, and shot great puffs of black smoke out of the stack, signaling its departure. Flaherty pulled Arthur up and over the edge of the canyon.

"My God, it's leaving us," Flaherty yelled. The fifty yards to the train was increasing as it chugged away. "The cattle car, grab on to the cattle car."

But the cattle car was slowing to a stop. They realized soldiers had released it to block the coming engine closing on them across the dry lake bed.

"The other one, Flaherty," Arthur ran and jumped on the coupling. He held out a hand to the Irishman who tripped on the rail ties. Arthur caught him by the shoulder, grabbing his suspenders which snapped, then caught his shirt and arm. They hung onto the slats of the cattle car. A heifer looked at them and snorted its disapproval. Pulling off one slat and kicking in another, they squeezed into the car with the complaining black cows, unhappy to have visitors. The two squeezed, pushed, and cursed their way forward.

"Horses don't smell this bad," shouted the Irishman over the groans of the cattle. Covered with sweat and cow dung, they found a door at the end and opened it as the train, gaining speed puffed out onto the bridge and crossed the dreaded canyon.

Behind, engine number 76 with its brass ringed funnel and church sized bell squealed to a stop with a furious

Colonel hanging out the cabin window, shaking his fist at the departing train leaving the bridge, out of range of his sharp-shooters.

The gringos, holding onto the cattle car, kicked on the locked door to the passenger car. After more kicking and yelling, two soldiers lifted the bar and opened the door, and the foreigners entered the car looking like two men returning from hell. They stood staggering, covered with the stinking dung, Flaherty with one suspender brace holding up his plaid pants, while the President's brother, his officers, and the family stared.

"Buenos tardes," muttered Arthur and they moved to their seats. Flaherty flashed a quick smile. The girls across the aisle were the first to move away, holding their noses. Arthur opened the window, but the incoming breeze made it worse.

"Just a few more hours, Johannesen. I can't wait to cross the Rio Grande again and be out of this mess."

Arthur took a deep breath. "Flaherty. Will you get the fruit? I'm hungry."

At the bridge, The *Express de Hidalgo del Parral,* inched forward and clanked onto the lonely cattle car and began to push. The Hawk with his niece and his sharpshooters, continued across the bridge, at only thirty miles-per-hour toward Juarez, in his strained pursuit of the Dos Gringos.

Chapter Twenty-five
Whew!

Oblivious to the gawking and snickering people on the platform at the Juarez station where they had left with higher expectations and cleaner clothes only three weeks before, Arthur politely asked a man, "Donde El Paso?" and they took off in the direction of his gesture.

"Hey, Flaherty." Arthur stopped at the center of the bridge over the Rio Grande. "This stuff means more to them than to us." He pointed to the score of boys in the knee deep waters of the river thirty feet below. "At least we have some money in the bank."

He opened his suitcase, dug in and sifted the bills into the hot breeze. The pesos, almost worthless in the dollar world of El Paso, floated like autumn leaves to the eager hands of the boys jumping in the muddy water to catch them.

"Not much in mine anymore," said Flaherty as he unlatched his case and the remainder of his pay followed the Norwegian's, some drifting over the boys and floating down stream.

"Did you keep something for a beer?" asked Arthur.

"Sure," and he pulled a few dollars out of his pocket.

"I knew I could count on you," said Arthur who put his arm around Flaherty's shoulders, as they headed for the Rio Grande Bar and Grill.

Two hours later, at the Juarez station, an unusual thing happened in front of the workers, soldiers, and passengers waiting for the train to Chihuahua, which was late this afternoon due to an unexpected delay. Another unscheduled train steamed into the station, the antique engine with a proud 76 visible under the grime of its cab. It was straining for lack of water, and pushing a cattle car ahead, hungry noses twisting between the slats. It braked to a screeching halt, but the cattle car uncoupled and rolled on, crashing onto the iron and log barrier at the end of the track by the platform. The side door slammed open. Black heads peered out the open door, mooing in amazement. Pushed from behind, hungry, stinking black cows poured onto the passenger platform, stumbling, swaying, and scattering the men, the ladies dropping their bundles in their flight, the soldiers running around the corner. Tacos and beans flew from the toppled food cart just arrived to feed the restless crowd. The cows raced through the station lobby, the clerks wide-eyed in disbelief. Tumbling into the street, screeching in their hunger and freedom, the cows scattered. The children laughed.

The Hawk had arrived.

Chapter Twenty-six
Unintended Consequences

"Ah, señores, welcome back," said Raimondo the bartender, the ever-present rag in his hand and a smile on his face. He sniffed the air and called, "Paco," and whispered a few words in the boy's ear. Paco motioned Flaherty and Arthur to follow him out the back door to the wash tub, gave them a bar of soap, a big brush, and one tattered towel. He pointed to the outhouse, pointed to their boots, shook his head, and held his nose.

When they reentered the saloon, a bit more acceptable in their wrinkled spare clothes, two beers were waiting for them on the bar.

"Nothing has changed, Johannesen," said Flaherty with a smile. He nodded to the end of the bar where the fat drunk was again asleep with his head on his chest.

"Nothing but you and me, my friend," Arthur said and he wiped his mouth on his sleeve.

"Señores," and the bartender pointed to a table where

Paco was placing two plates of hot roast beef and green beans. It was the same table where Ayles had said, "Trust me," a few weeks before. They looked at each other, and then at the bartender with their outturned palms to indicate they couldn't pay.

"Later, señores, later." The bartender smiled. "You see Mr. Ayles?"

They laughed. "Ayles?" Arthur said and they shook their heads in dismay. "Who knows where Mr. Ayles is now."

Mopping his plate with a biscuit, Arthur said, "I think we are home, Flaherty."

After an hour and more beers, the swinging doors banged open and all talk and motion stopped. In the doorway where weeks ago stood an Easterner looking to hire a couple of men for an easy job with "no danger," now stood a Mexican in a Stetson and with two pearl handled Colts. It was El Halcyon, "The Hawk," three of his soldiers with long rifles, his niece Luisa, and a priest.

"Good evening, amigos." His hand was on his revolver. Customers began to slip out the back door.

"Hello, Michael," said Luisa, a coy smile on her face.

"Is this the man, Luisa?" her uncle asked. "The only red-haired man in Mexico?"

"Sí, Uncle Marcus, this is my friend," she said and tipped her head and smiled.

"You have put me to great trouble, Irishman."

Flaherty sat silent; his heart racing like it was trying to escape. His eyes flashed to Arthur, the bartender, the guitar player.

Arthur bent over to him, shaking his head and whispered, "A wise man told me once, when it comes to love, secrets don't keep."

Waving his pistol, The Hawk said, "I picked up a priest in Juarez, in case you admit your involvement with my dear niece." He pointed the gun at Flaherty. "And if you deny it…" The Hawk cocked his pistol with his thumb. "…Father Oswaldo, he performs weddings and funerals, same price."

Flaherty felt like someone had turned up the heat.

"So what do you say, Irishman?"

Luisa leaned to Flaherty. "I am sorry for all this," she said, "but it will be all right. Tell my uncle what you told me, Michael. That I was the kind of woman you always wanted."

"Well, well, that's the truth, but—"

"You were right, my dear," The Hawk said to his niece with a smile, and he turned to Flaherty.

Flaherty finally found enough strength to stand up. He looked at Arthur, expecting something, but Arthur could only shrug in his helplessness.

"Then you are a man of honor, Irishman," Luisa's uncle said. "I am glad to hear that." He used his Colt as a pointer like he was giving a lecture. "Father Oswaldo, let's do what is necessary now, and we will find a church tomorrow."

Flaherty looked at Arthur again.

"You could do worse my friend. You have no choice it looks like. They are strict about those things. She's Catholic, yes?"

"She is pretty nice. Those eyes," said Flaherty.

The priest gathered his robe, pulled out a book from his bag, took Luisa's arm, and moved her beside Flaherty. He said some things in Latin, then in Spanish, then in English, asked them to kneel, and with a gold crucifix from his bag made the sign of the cross over their heads. He had first the groom and then the bride kiss the cross, and pronounced them husband and wife. That was it. Michael Flaherty turned pale and Luisa helped him to stand.

"Que bueno! Que bueno!" said the bartender. *"Felicitaciónes a todos. Cerveza por todos,"* and he started filling the mugs and everyone clapped and laughed and started singing.

Even Flaherty smiled, blinked his eyes, took a beer, and had the wise inspiration to toast his new uncle, The Hawk.

Young Paco tugged on his father's sleeve. "Papa, there is a lady at the door."

The bartender looked over the happy crowd and went to see what she wanted, a pretty brown-haired lady with hazel eyes and a nice smile.

"Is a Mr. Arthur Johannesen here in your tavern?" she asked.

"Maybe, señorita," he said, afraid to commit himself and looking back into the boisterous room and waving his rag.

"Maybe, come look, *por favor.*"

Pauline Müller stepped into the room and immediately pointed to Arthur. "That's him."

Arthur looked quite happy, swinging his beer mug to a Mexican song he didn't know.

She moved over into his sight and waved her hand to catch his attention.

He stopped, his face in shock, spilling his beer. He slid the mug onto the bar and hurried to the door.

"Pauline! How did you know?" he said. "I just got here."

She smiled. "Small town." She shrugged and took his hand. They embraced and kissed. She rubbed his face with her hand. "You need a shave."

"What a happy thing," he said. "Come meet my friends," and he put his hand on the door to close it, but she held back.

"First," she said, "someone is with me I want you to meet."

"Oh. Sure, you bet."

Out of the dark stepped a man. He was tall, in a black suit with a pointed white handkerchief in his breast pocket. On his head he wore a homburg. He smiled under his thin mustache.

"I would like you to meet my father, Mr. Müller." She smiled back and forth between them, and Arthur stood, his mouth half open.

Arthur felt a chill, his words caught deep inside.

Friedrich Müller held out his hand, not surprised at Arthur's shock.

"You—" stuttered Arthur, "—you, you are Pauline's father? And you—" he pointed across the border, "are—"

Pauline was stunned. "What are you saying, Arthur?"

"Yes," Müller said. "Shall we go inside?"

Friedrich Müller of Krakauer, Zork, and Moye, was not known to anyone there except The Hawk, and they shook hands like classmates.

Pauline held Arthur tight. "I don't know what this is all about," she said, "but I am so happy you are safe."

Arthur melted from the sparkle in her eyes.

"Father said he will give you a job at Zork's. No more Mexico."

Arthur, now very sober, looked at his future father-in-law and smiled. "I, I don't know."

"Don't worry," Müller said, "they need a man good with machines."

"I think we have some things to discuss," said Arthur.

"There are no secrets," said Müller, "but first things first. You need a job."

Arthur pointed at the floor below him. "But on this side of the Rio Grande."

"Of course," Müller said, "I wouldn't allow it any other way."

The party was over for the gringos.

Mr. and Mrs. Michael Flaherty left, he with a multi-beer smile on his face, and she with a firm grip on his arm.

Arthur Johannesen and his bride-to-be left with her gun-selling father to the waiting Model-T.

"I have kept my promise, Pauline," Arthur said.

"That is why I love you, Arthur. But first," she said, "I think you must have a bath."

Chapter Twenty-seven
"I do, you bet."

On the open front doors of the Zion Evangelical Lutheran Church, Missouri Synod, on Pershing Drive, hung large wreathes of roses, one red and one white. It was a Sunday afternoon, October 16, 1916.

The church, built to serve the influx of German Lutherans that had migrated from the San Antonio area and before that from the Rhineland, was of red brick, with a flat-topped crenellated tower like a medieval fortress. Three tall arched windows of stained glass identified it as a church. A smiling man in a tuxedo welcomed the guests to the wedding, and formally passed them to the ushers who held out a tuxedoed arm, asking if they were there for the bride or for the groom.

In a small room behind a door sat Pauline and her father, ready for her walk to Mendelssohn's music. She adjusted her flowered tiara in the mirror.

"You have chosen a good man, my dear," Friedrich Müller said and kissed her on the cheek. "I don't say this only to calm a nervous daughter." An attendant straightened the folds of Pauline's train as they approached the door, poised and waiting for the signal. "I saw and heard plenty of him in Mexico," he said, "so I know he will stand by you and be a good father. He is strong and determined."

"I do love him," she said. She smiled and squeezed her father's hand. "He is funny when you get to know him, and so thoughtful."

"We will all get to know him, my dear."

If friends of the Müllers, the ushers escorted the visitors to the seats on the left, and if friends of Arthur Johannesen, then on the right. By a minute before three o'clock the left side of the church had forty-seven sitting there, and on the right, there were twelve.

The Müller side included Pauline's mother Charlotte, Pauline's sister Milda, and friends from the Kelleher, Freiburger, and other families. Also there was Adolphe Schwartz, representing that prominent Jewish family which controlled much of the higher-end retail business in El Paso and friend of the Krakauers. Messers Zork and Moye were in the third row.

On the Johannesen side was Chris Yokum, Arthur's new supervisor at Zork's, and his wife, Gertrude, and some other new friends from Zork's heavy machine department. In the first row Luisa Flaherty, in a maternity dress, was next to her two mustachioed men in American suits, white shirts, and narrow ties. Next to one of these Villistas was a tall gray-streaked blond woman with a big smile. She turned to Luisa's Villista friend, and said to him in Norwegian, "Isn't she beautiful? I am so proud of my son." The man nodded politely. Arthur's mother had caught one of the ships of Captain Johannesen's company and raced to America as she had not seen her son for over two years. "Arthur has always had good taste," she said to the man.

In the second row, dressed in white shirts and ties was Raimondo Escobar, wife Yolanda, and his son Paco from the Rio Grande Café and Bar and a few of their friends. Behind them was a surprise guest, in a gray suit, white shirt, tie, and a fresh haircut. It was Wolfgang Heinz, smiling.

Mendelssohn's Wedding March began, all heads turned to see Pauline, beaming in her gold-trimmed white dress and train, gold ornaments in her brown locks under the tiara. Locked onto the arm of her tuxedoed father, the two walked slowly up the aisle, returning the smiles of the guests. He whispered to her, "Don't trip."

Meeting the bride and her father at the altar was Arthur and his best man, Michael Flaherty, fidgeting with the ring pillow. He managed to give the ring to Arthur to slip onto Pauline's slender finger. The minister of Zion Lutheran, Dr. Arnold Kraus read from the Bible; Isaiah, Psalms, Second Corinthians and talked of marriage being a journey, about trials, forgiveness and love reflected in love.

The two, their eyes glistening with happiness, committed themselves to love, cherish, and obey, to care for each other, and to be faithful until death do them part. When asked for their commitment, Pauline said, "Yes, forever," and Arthur answered, "Ja," then turned to the minister, nodded his head and added, "I promise, you bet." Minister Kraus pronounced them man and wife. They kissed.

Chapter Twenty-eight
All's Well

The scent of flowers filled the air of the Müller home on Raynor Street, not far from the Lutheran Church. Roses, chrysanthemums, and sunflowers from the garden were in a bouquet on every table. The mother of the bride, in her pink and white organdy dress, met the guests with a big smile. Although a short woman, she was clearly in control of every detail of the wedding reception. The party was held in the parlor opening onto the spacious back yard. Everyone from church was there and more.

The reception line of well-wishers preceded the food, prepared by Mrs. Müller and neighbors. Smoked pork ribs with sauerkraut and olive tortilla pinwheels reflected the mixed culture of El Paso.

Arthur and Mrs. Johannesen, the smiling mother from Norway, posed with the bride for photos, the flash blinding. Arthur was delighted to have someone to speak Norwegian with.

After the first courses, Arthur strolled over to Heinz, who stood in the corner by the weeping willow, a plate of German sausage rolls and a glass of wine in his hands. He said to the German, "Ja, Heinz, what a surprise to see you north of the Rio Grande—and welcome."

"With your father-in-law's help at the border."

"Well, Pauline is the most beautiful woman in Texas, I tell you that," Arthur said.

On this day, the highlight of the groom's life, he gave not a thought to anything about Norway. Even the Mexican escapade of a few months prior was a disconnected past. Arthur didn't know what to say to the man, who had both shot at him and saved his life, but he was learning to leave it at that.

"Now," Heinz said, "we are all just hard-working men. I have a woman at home, too. I hope to see her someday soon."

"So you will be going back to Germany?"

"This game in Mexico isn't working," said Heinz.

"Soon," said Arthur, "America will be in the war. It has to be. Then we may be enemies?"

"Our countries may be enemies if that happens, Arthur, but I hope not you and me."

Arthur offered his hand, "Ja, we should shake on that."

"And," said Heinz, "here comes your Irish Best Man."

Flaherty shook the German's hand and looked about the yard. "It looks like all we lack now is Mr. Smythe."

"That won't be possible," Heinz said. "Smythe was called back to England. He was tired of spying on me."

Flaherty stood quiet for a moment. "I hope he is safe, I

do. And Heinz, what about Tomás?"

"He sent his blessings to you both. He is caring for his grandfather who's about gone. Tomás will be all right."

Torches were lit in the garden as the sun sank behind the Franklin Mountains.

"Gentlemen, come," called Müller, "this is not the time for international intrigue."

"But the war is a worry," said Flaherty. "The paper said a million men lost in that Somme battle. I can't imagine that. What stupidity—on both sides."

"But no Americans," said Müller.

Flaherty paused. "Yet."

"But the mine, Heinz," asked Arthur, "what about the mine?"

"Nothing has changed since you left when Ayles kicked out the prop, and it all came to a smoking halt."

Arthur shook his head in disgust. "It wouldn't have lasted anyway. It was all pretend."

"And Ayles?" asked Flaherty.

"No idea," said Heinz. "Never heard from him again."

Prancing up to them, Pauline, clapped her hands and said, "Gentlemen, what are you doing here? Come Arthur, it's time for the cake cutting."

"Ja vell, the cake. Important."

"Most important," said Flaherty.

"No, not most important," said Arthur. "Most important comes tonight. Hotel Paso del Norte. This time, the bridal suite."

Epilogue

While the Mexican Revolution dragged on, the Johannesen and the Flaherty families settled into the safety north of the border. Arthur worked at Krakauer, Zork, and Moye for two years where he was during the war when twenty-four million men were registered for duty in Europe. Even as an alien he was susceptible for draft into the Army. The war was over before his name came up, younger single men being taken first. He and Pauline began a family which eventually included four children. Arthur later joined El Paso Natural Gas Company, which discovered gas in Texas and piped it to California. He managed the largest machine shop in the West, invented the pressure-weld system, and was in charge of the giant Cooper-Bessemer compressor engines from Texas to California.

Michael Flaherty was called up to serve in the Army because the authorities at first did not recognize his El Paso saloon marriage and subsequent Juarez church wedding.

But he was assigned to Fort Bliss in El Paso training the new cavalrymen on how to raise and care for their horses. He and Luisa raised a family which eventually grew to seven children. Flaherty and his children later owned and ran a horse farm on the Rio Grande near Ysleta, south of El Paso.

Tomás heeded the advice of the gringos, went to college once things settled down after the Revolution, and became a professor of history and government at the University of Chihuahua. The Hawk became a politico and lived a long and prosperous life. Ayles, on his return from La Promesa, stayed at the Hotel Centrál in Jimenez, and after being seduced by Mrs. Townes, married her and decided to stay in Mexico and help run the hotel.

Author's Comments

Some years ago, at a table in a Mexican restaurant in Phoenix, my septuagenarian father told me this story of his escapades in the Mexican Revolution. I was born and raised in El Paso and close to my dad, but I had never heard this story before and wondered what else he never told me. I had him repeat the tale several times and recorded it. Of course, details changed as his memory or imagination caught fire. In the story, some names have been created to fit the characters who are all real, including the mysterious man selling guns to both sides, my grandfather for whom I am named (re: the Zimmerman telegram.) But, the story you have read happened more or less as presented.

Frederick R. Andresen
Corona del Mar, California